EZRA, NEHEMIAH, AND ESTHER

PRINCIPLES FOR VICTORY OVER FAILURE

Ezra, Nehemiah, and Esther

Principles For Victory Over Failure

F. Wayne Mac Leod

Authentic
MEDIA

Contents

Esther

Preface

Ezra is the story of a priest whose God-given vision was to see the restoration of the temple of God and its worship in the nation of Israel. The prophecy of Ezra was written at a time when Israel was returning from exile in Babylon. Ezra shows us how a sovereign God was able to move in the hearts of pagan kings and use them as instruments to restore his people to their homeland. This prophecy reveals the challenges God's people had to face in order to restore godly worship in their land. Ezra himself had to overcome false expectations, discouragement, and deteriorating relationships in his efforts to see God's people reestablish the entire system of Jewish ritual. While this seemed like an impossible task, God used his servant Ezra to move his people from discouragement to tremendous revival.

Nehemiah, like Ezra, returned to Jerusalem from exile in Babylon. Nehemiah organized God's people to rebuild the city wall around Jerusalem. He too faced both opposition from the enemy and clashes among the people of God.

Personally attacked and criticized, Nehemiah relied on the Lord God. In the Lord's strength and wisdom, Nehemiah led God's people to victory and the completion of the wall. His heart, like that of Ezra, was to see a people living in harmony with the plan and purpose of the Lord God in the land he had given them. Nehemiah reminds us that with trust and confident obedience there is nothing God calls us to do that is impossible.

The book of Esther shows us how a sovereign God can take simple people and use them to accomplish his wonderful purpose in a nation. Esther was a relatively unknown individual who was empowered and blessed by God to be an instrument of his salvation for an entire nation. The book also shows us how God can take the efforts of the enemy and use them to accomplish his glory in our lives. In the book of Esther we see that there is purpose and meaning in all that happens. You will be comforted and encouraged as you see God working on behalf of his people.

These books speak of victory through perseverance and obedience. They show us what God is able to do through all who will persevere in obedient faith. The faithful individuals we meet in these books are inspirational to anyone who wants to live a life of victory. They give us courage to keep going. I trust that you will be blessed as much as I have been in preparing this manuscript.

Take the time to work slowly through these books. Be sure to read the Bible passage noted at the beginning of each chapter. On completion of the chapter, take a moment to answer the questions for consideration. End your time with prayer, asking God to apply the truths of these passages to your life.

My prayer is that in some way this devotional commentary will have an impact on your spiritual walk. I have often felt unworthy of this task, but take courage in what I have discovered in these books. God is able to overcome even the strongest obstacle through simple human beings who step out in faith and obedience. This commentary is a step of faith and obedience. I trust that God will bless you through it and use it to strengthen you in your walk with him.

F. Wayne Mac Leod

Ezra

1

The Proclamation
of Cyrus

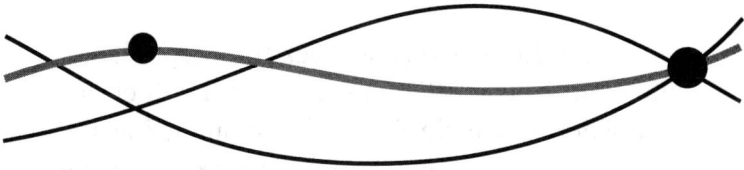

Read Ezra 1:1–11

A s we begin a brief study of the book of Ezra, we need to take a moment to consider its historical context. God's people were in exile in Babylon because of their sin. For many years they had been dominated by Assyria, Babylon, and then Persia. Politically, the dominant power of this time was Persia, under the leadership of King Cyrus.

The book begins in the first year of the reign of King Cyrus when he made an astounding proclamation. He announced that the God of heaven had commissioned him to build a temple in Jerusalem (verse 2). Why would the God of Israel speak to a pagan king and commission him to this task? Why would a pagan king be interested in building a temple in Jerusalem to the God of Israel? As unbelievable as this sounds, Ezra reminded his people that Jeremiah the prophet had prophesied this event many years before. Jeremiah had spoken of a time of exile from the land of

Israel and prophesied that after seventy years, God's people would return from that captivity and rebuild their temple and the city of Jerusalem.

> When seventy years are completed for Babylon, I will come to you and fulfill my gracious promise to bring you back to this place. For I know the plans I have for you, declares the LORD, plans to prosper you and not to harm you, plans to give you hope and a future. (Jeremiah 29:10–11)

> I will bring Judah and Israel back from captivity and will rebuild them as they were before. I will cleanse them from all the sin they have committed against me and will forgive all their sins of rebellion against me. Then this city will bring me renown, joy, praise and honor before all nations on earth that hear of all the good things I do for it; and they will be in awe and will tremble at the abundant prosperity and peace I provide for it. (Jeremiah 33:7–9)

God's ways are not the same as ours. God moved the heart of King Cyrus to open the door for his people to return to their land. Cyrus was very likely the last person in the world God's people would have expected to facilitate the fulfillment of Jeremiah's prophecy. In our time of need, the Lord brings help from strange and unexpected sources.

Notice also that God is not bound to use his people only. He can even use the unbeliever or anything else he desires to accomplish his purposes. In the days of the prophet Jonah, God used a pagan ship captain to rebuke the prophet for his refusal to pray (Jonah 1:6). In Numbers 22:26–30 God used Balaam's donkey to show him the error of his ways. Cyrus had a very clear sense of the call of God on his life for this specific task. We need to examine several points about the proclamation that Cyrus made concerning Israel.

Notice first that Cyrus was aware that the God of heaven had given him all the kingdoms of the earth (verse 2). Cyrus was a very powerful king, but he did not take credit for his accomplishments. Though his armies had conquered many nations, Cyrus understood that without the Lord's help, he would never have been successful.

Our God gives this world to whomever he sees fit. He is king of all kings. God does not bless the believer only. His hand also reaches out to the unbeliever. Unlike King Cyrus, however, many people do not give glory and recognition to God as the source of all they have.

The God who gave these nations to Cyrus then called him to release the Jews from his bondage. God gives but he also takes away. As a sovereign God, he has the right to do with his creation as he pleases. Notice that not only did God expect Cyrus to release his people but he also expected him to enable them financially.

It is important for us to see in verse 2 how God led Cyrus to put all these things down in writing. While this may not appear to be of significance at this point in the story, it proves to be very important later. Because of this written proclamation of Cyrus, orders were issued to the enemies of God's people, commanding them to stop opposing the construction of the city and temple (Ezra 5–6). Even in the matter of writing down the proclamation, God had a purpose and plan.

In verse 3 Cyrus issues a command for the Jews to return to their homeland to rebuild the temple of God in Jerusalem. We understand from Haggai 1:3-4 that the people who returned from exile also built their own houses at this time. Cyrus blessed them in their return and commissioned them to rebuild the temple. King Cyrus also commanded that inhabitants of his dominion open their hearts and provide the silver, gold, and goods necessary to accomplish this task.

God moved the heart of King Cyrus. Next God moved the hearts of his own people. Jews from various tribes felt the call of God to return to Jerusalem to take up the king's challenge. When God has a work to do, he moves in the hearts of his people to do that work. He also opens doors so that his people will lack nothing to do what he has called them to do. We can trust him to provide all that is necessary to complete that task. This is part of his call. He will provide the resources to do what he has called us to do. We can step out in confidence.

From across the Persian Empire, resources began to pour in for the work of the temple in Jerusalem. People whose hearts were moved donated articles of silver and gold. The neighbors of the Jews gave them goods and livestock. Cyrus returned to the Jews the articles taken from the temple in Jerusalem by Nebuchadnezzar seventy years before. These articles had been stored in the pagan temple of the god of Nebuchadnezzar in Babylon.

God is in the business of restoring those things the enemy has taken from us. Christians all over this world are battling the enemy. While the Lord has already conquered Satan on the cross, each of us has experienced lost battles. Maybe as you look at your own Christian life, you are aware of how much the enemy has taken from you. Maybe you have suffered a broken relationship. Maybe your walk with God is not where it should be. The church is filled with wounded soldiers. Like the Jews of Ezra's day, we have not always lived in obedience and now suffer the consequences of our actions. Here we meet a God who restores the treasures God's people had lost to the enemy. What an encouragement this ought to be to us today.

Under the direction of Mithredath, the Persian treasurer, an inventory was taken of the restored articles. In all, there were 5,400 articles of gold and silver returned to Israel. It was as if these articles had been kept for the people of God, waiting for the appropriate time. When the time was right, these blessings were poured out. What does God have in store for us? What blessings await us as we step out in obedience to that call of God on our hearts to rebuild his temple in this world?

What we need to see here is that the God who calls us will also equip us to do the work he has called us to do. The God who called his people to rebuild the ruined temple opened hearts and prepared the way for this to take place. He went before his people. God's people could step out in confidence. We too can have that same confidence.

For Consideration:

• What kind of people does God use in this chapter?

• What does God do for those who step out in obedience to his call in this chapter?

• What has the Lord God put on your heart to do? What encouragement and challenge do you receive from this chapter?

• What keeps you from stepping out in obedience to the Lord today?

• What has the enemy taken from you over the past few years? What encouragement do you receive from the fact that God is a God who delights in restoring what the enemy has taken from us?

For Prayer:

• Thank the Lord that when he calls he also provides all that is necessary to fulfill that calling.

- Ask the Lord to restore what the enemy has taken from you.

- Ask the Lord to give you boldness to step out in belief and confidence in him.

2

The People Who Returned

Read Ezra 2:1–70

We often wonder why the Lord saw fit to include long lists of names and numbers in Scripture. Ezra 2 contains one of these lists. There are, however, some key devotional insights we need to see in this list.

In chapter 2 we have a lengthy list of names. The names on this list are the names of those Israelites who first returned to Jerusalem from the Babylonian captivity. Some seventy years before the writing of this list, King Nebuchadnezzar of Babylon had conquered Judah and taken many captives to his empire in Babylon. (Babylon had been subsequently conquered by Persia.) Many on this list had only heard about Jerusalem. They were not old enough to remember the temple and the once-glorious city. While many had never seen the temple in Jerusalem, the Lord had put a burden on their hearts to see it rebuilt (1:5).

These listed individuals traveled from the Persian Empire to Jerusalem with Zerubbabel (the rightful Jewish leader of Judah) and Jeshua (the high priest). The leader named Nehemiah mentioned here is not the same man spoken of in Nehemiah 1:1 who later returned to Jerusalem with another group of exiles. While Ezra was not in this first group of returning exiles, we know that the Lord later called him to be a leader among these people. We have already seen that God provided the resources necessary for the completion of the task in Jerusalem. Here the Lord also provides his willing servants a team of solid leaders to direct them. Leadership is important to God.

We can only imagine the excitement that was in the air as these Israelites prepared to leave the land of their captivity. This was the start of something new for them. God was calling out a team of people to restore Jerusalem and to spread the light of truth to the world. What an honor it was to be part of that team.

Notice in verse 2 that the list is composed of men only. We can assume, however, that there were also women and children who returned. It was typical for the Jews of this time to record the names of men only as the heads of their families. This list is divided into descendants. Family lines were very important to the Jews of that day. We will not spend the time here to repeat the names listed in this section.

Note in this list the reference to the various offices held by these returning exiles. Among those present in this list were priests (verse 36), Levites (verse 40), singers (verse 41), gatekeepers (verse 42), and temple servants (verse 43). We cannot help but notice how the hand of God was putting this team together. These individuals had different functions in the rebuilding of the temple. They had different gifts and callings. God made no mistake when he put this team together. He had a specific task for each person in the work of rebuilding. The same is true for us today. We all have roles to play and gifts to use. God does not call each of us to the same task. He does not give us all the same gifts or offices. We are dependant on each other. Only as these gifts and callings flow together can the work be accomplished.

There are two other things we need to note in this list. First, verse 59 tells about certain individuals from the towns of Tel Melah, Tel Harsha, Kerub, Addon and Immer. These individuals came with the people of God, but it could not be shown from the records that they truly were Israelites. These facts were noted on the list. It is hard to say why these individuals came with the group that returned from exile. Maybe they had their own personal motives. Maybe they had been touched by the witness of the Jews in exile. We simply do not know. The reality of the matter is that in any given church or ministry, there is always the possibility of finding those who are not really children of God. People are involved in ministry for various reasons. Not all who minister are called of God. I am not saying that the individuals recorded in this passage were not called of God. There was, however, some question regarding whether they were children of God. We need to take this as a warning. The enemy has always sent his servants among God's people to hinder the work God wants to do.

The second point we need to see is in verses 61-63. Also on the list were those who claimed to be priests but whose line could not be established. Their call to the priesthood was uncertain. These individuals were excluded from the work of the priesthood. They were not to eat the sacred food or minister until their calling was sure. This would be determined by means of a priest ministering with the Urim and Thummim

We read in Exodus 28:30 that the priest was to carry the Urim and Thummim in his breastpiece when he went into the presence of the Lord. These articles were very likely special stones used to determine the will of God. It is unclear how these stones would indicate the will of God or exactly how they were used. By means of these stones, however, the Lord would communicate his purpose and will to his priests.

Again, the warning is that that there are those who come to minister to us who are not truly called. It is quite possible for us to minister in areas where we are not called to minister. How easy it is to look at someone else's ministry and so admire them that we want to be just like them though we do not have their calling. Those whom God had established as leaders among the returning exiles wanted to be sure of the call of those who ministered among them. The concern of the leaders was to oversee the will of God accomplished by only the chosen servants of God. Those who could not clearly demonstrate that call of God were asked to refrain.

What a challenge this is for us as church leaders as well. Are those teaching Sunday School in your church truly called of God to do so? Are the elders, deacons, or committee members of your church called to that ministry? We can learn a very important lesson here. We can only truly advance the kingdom if those who are ministering are specifically called to minister.

As this great team arrived in Jerusalem, they numbered 42,360 plus servants as well as a large number of cattle (verses 64–67). The Lord put it on the hearts of some of these families to give a freewill offering for the rebuilding of the temple of God. These individuals gave as the Lord enabled them so that the work could be accomplished. Verse 69 tells us that they gave 61,000 drachmas of gold. This would be approximately 1,100 pounds or 500 kilograms. The people also gave 5,000 minas of silver (approximately 3 tons) and 100 priestly garments. These were substantial gifts. God was moving in the hearts of his people. He had great plans for the city of Jerusalem.

God's hand was on the returning exiles. He provided the resources necessary for them to accomplish the task of rebuilding the temple. The Lord also gave them a team of solid leaders so that the work would move ahead smoothly. Those who led God's people were specifically called and equipped for leadership. God also moved in the hearts of his people to give them a spirit of generosity. God's people could expect great things from their Lord.

For Consideration:

- What does this passage teach us about how God puts together people of different gifts and talents for the work of extending the kingdom?

- How important is it that we know the call of God on our lives?

- Is everyone who seeks to minister called to that ministry? What does this passage teach us about this issue?

- What do we learn here about the importance of leadership in the work of the kingdom?

- What is the call of God on your life?

For Prayer:

- Ask the Lord to help you to know his call on your life.

- Thank the Lord that he has given to the church individuals with various gifts and callings to complement others in the work of ministry.

- Ask the Lord to help you to be content with his call on your life. Ask him to enable you to complement your brothers and sisters in the ministry of the expansion of his kingdom.

3

Construction Begins

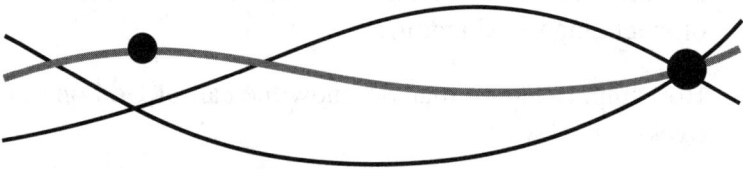

Read Ezra 3:1–13

In the last chapter, we examined the list of God's people who returned from exile to rebuild the temple in Jerusalem. The rebuilding team had arrived in Israel and was settled in various towns. In the seventh month, they assembled in the city of Jerusalem, very likely for the celebration of the Feast of Tabernacles as described in Leviticus 23:39-43.

Notice that verse 1 tells us that the Israelites assembled "as one man." This is an indication of the unity of the team that God had called to rebuild the temple. There was joy and excitement in the air. These people had a clear vision and were unified in that vision. They wanted to see the temple rebuilt and the city of Jerusalem restored to its former glory.

The first item on the agenda was the construction of an altar for the sacrifice of burnt offerings. It was Jeshua, the high priest, and his fellow priests who undertook the responsibility to build this altar (verse 2). They built it according to the specifications God had given to Moses in the Law (Exodus 38). It is of significance that the altar was the first item on the agenda. The altar was the place where offerings were made for sin. Those who were involved in the work of rebuilding the temple needed to be a forgiven and pure people. Before moving ahead with the construction of the temple, they needed to get right with God.

Building the altar was not without its difficulties. Verse 3 tells us that the Israelites were afraid of the people around them. Even at this early stage, there was evidence of opposition to the rebuilding work God wanted to do in Israel. We can be sure that when the Lord wants to move ahead, the enemy will never be far behind, seeking to discourage those who take on the challenge. Though they were fearful of what their enemies might do, the priests placed their confidence in God and forged ahead. The result was that the altar was completed and sacrifices were offered to the Lord both day and night.

Also in accordance with the Law of Moses in Leviticus 23:42–43, the returned exiles celebrated the Feast of Tabernacles (verse 4). During this celebration the Israelites would leave their homes and live in small booths made from branches. The Israelites placed these booths in their courtyards, on the roofs of their homes, or anywhere they could find a place to set them up. They did this to remember the time when their ancestors lived in similar booths when wandering through the wilderness. During this celebration sacrifices were made each day. The Israelites remembered at this time the goodness of the Lord to them not only in rescuing them from the land of Egypt but now also from the land of their exile in Babylon.

Verse 7 tells us that during this time, money was given to the masons and carpenters to begin the work of rebuilding the temple. Notice also that food, drink, and oil was sent to the people of Sidon and Tyre so that they would bring logs by sea from Lebanon and Joppa. These were exciting times for the people of God. Sacrifices were again being offered and the work of rebuilding the temple was getting under way. It was in the second month of the second year that Zerubbabel, the priest, commissioned Levites twenty years of age and older to supervise the building of the temple of the Lord (verse 8).

In the course of time, the builders laid the foundation of the temple. When the foundation was completed, the people gathered for a time of celebration. Verse 10 tells us that the priests dressed in their priestly garments with trumpets in hand. The Levites were present with cymbals. Together they took their places and began to sing praises to the Lord according to the instruction of King David. They glorified the Lord for the work that had been accomplished. They sang of the goodness and love of the God of Israel. The people joined the Levites and priests in celebration and thanksgiving.

We should remember that the altar had been built despite the fear of their enemies. The thanksgiving offered here was to a God who had enabled them to build the foundation despite the opposition of the enemy around them. It must have been exciting to see how the Lord God was with them in those days. Not only was he providing the money necessary for the construction but he was also holding back their enemies.

Those present that day realized that none of this would have been possible were it not for the Lord God. There is an important reminder for us in this thought. Where would we be today were it not for the Lord? As we look at our achievements and accomplishments in this world, do we realize, as those gathered around the temple's foundation, that we owe everything to the Lord God? Do our hearts leap for joy and thanksgiving to the God who made all our achievements possible?

We need to understand that when the Lord is active, the enemy is never very far behind. Sometimes the enemy comes in unexpected ways. As this worship and thanksgiving was being offered to the Lord God, the older people who had seen the former temple were very displeased. They wept aloud while the younger people rejoiced and praised the Lord with thanksgiving.

We need to take a moment to consider what was happening here. Those who had been in Israel some seventy years prior to this event had seen the glory of the former temple. As they looked at this temple's foundation, they realized that it was not going to be as big and as glorious as the former temple. The prophet Haggai described the thoughts of the older generation of that day: "Speak to Zerubbabel son of Shealtiel, governor of Judah, to Joshua son of Jehozadak, the high priest, and to the remnant of the people. Ask them, 'Who of you is left who saw this house in its former glory? How does it look to you now? Does it not seem to you like nothing?'" (Haggai 2:1–3).

On that day there was a mixture of emotion. The older generation could not see how this temple could ever be as glorious as the former temple. The younger generation, who had never seen the former temple, was simply excited to see what God was doing. The sounds of praise and the sounds of weeping rose together to God and were heard far away.

We can only wonder what that sound was like in the ears of God. Praise and grumbling do not seem to mix, yet this is what rose before God that day. The people of God had been successful in thwarting the plans and efforts of their unbelieving enemies around them. This attack of the enemy was more subtle. This time the enemy attacked from within. The discontent of the older generation could very easily become a discouragement to the younger generation.

When the enemy cannot defeat us by means of unbelievers, he will not hesitate to attack us from within. How often has the work of God been hindered by attacks from within? This is the first sign in this book of trouble in the body. The unity of the team that God had brought from exile was being threatened.

This passage challenges us to examine our own lives. God's ways are not like our ways. The challenge for us here is to let God do things in his way. The foundation was not what the older generation wanted, but it was what God wanted. We need to get our own ideas out of the way and surrender to what God wants to do. We must be careful lest our own ideas and plans destroy the unity of the team that God has been forming. The enemy had been trying to bring division to the team that God was forming. If he had succeeded in doing so, he would have been successful in hindering what God was doing in the land.

For Consideration:

• Have you been opposed in your ministry? What encouragement do you receive from this passage in seeing how the work of God progressed despite opposition?

• Take a moment to examine the things God has enabled you to accomplish in your life and ministry. Where would you be without God?

• What does this passage tell us about the way in which Satan attacks the work of God?

• Are there things that God is blessing around you that you have problems accepting? What are they? What does this passage teach us about dealing with these things?

For Prayer:

- Thank the Lord for the way he blesses and keeps us despite the many attacks of the enemy to keep us frustrated.

- Take a moment to examine what you have accomplished in ministry to this point. Thank the Lord that he has given you all these blessings. Confess to the Lord that without him none of this would be possible.

- Ask the Lord to forgive you for the times you have failed to bless what he has blessed. Ask him to give you a greater appreciation of the many different ways in which he works.

4

A Letter to King Artaxerxes

Read Ezra 4:1–24

One of the things we know about our enemy Satan is that he does not give up in his attempts to discourage believers in the work that God has called them to do. In the last chapter, he attacked by causing discontent in the hearts of the older Israelites who were not pleased with the size of the foundation of the new temple. This could have been a source of discouragement and disharmony for the rebuilding team. We see in this chapter that Satan also uses another means to attack God's people.

When the enemies of Judah and Benjamin heard of the rebuilding of the temple, they approached with what appeared to be a friendly gesture. The enemy offered to help in the rebuilding project. The enemy can be very subtle in his attacks. He often comes to us as a wolf in sheep's clothing. His attacks are sometimes disguised in acts of kindness and friendship.

In Acts 5 a couple by the name of Ananias and Sapphira came to the apostles with a gift of money from the sale of a piece of property. What was unseen to the human eye was the fact that this couple had secretly plotted to deceive the church by pretending that this gift was the complete sale price of the sold property. In reality, they had kept a portion for themselves. They were introducing deceit into the church. God struck them dead for their dishonesty. What looked to be so innocent on the outside was really the effort of the enemy to infiltrate the church with treachery. We see a similar thing happening here in the request of the enemies to help God's people with rebuilding the temple.

Notice in verse 2 that the enemies told Zerubbabel that they too sought the Lord God. They told him that they had been sacrificing to the Lord for many years. To understand what they were saying, we need to look at 2 Kings 17:24–29. In these verses we see that when the Assyrians conquered Israel many years before, they removed all the skilled laborers from the land and took them to Assyria. Only the poor and unskilled had remained in Israel. In 2 Kings 17:24 we see that the Assyrian king sent people from a variety of other conquered lands to live in Israel in the absence of the captured Israelites. These foreigners did not understand the ways of the Lord and did not serve him. The Lord was angry with them and sent lions to devour them. When this news reached the king of Assyria, he sent an Israelite priest back to Israel to teach the foreigners there the ways of the Lord of Israel. While these settlers did learn to sacrifice to the Lord God of Israel, they never quit worshiping their familiar idols. In 2 Kings 17:29 we learn that these foreigners sacrificed to the Lord God and also to their own gods. Eventually, these foreign settlers intermarried with some of the local Israelites, forming the Samaritan race. An intense bitterness grew between the Samaritans and the true Israelites who considered the Samaritans as unclean because they were of mixed blood and mixed beliefs (see John 4). Here in our passage, it is the Samaritans who were asking to help the returned exiles in the reconstruction of the temple.

Zerubbabel listened to the Samaritans' request but refused to let them help. It is hard for us to know the intentions of these enemies, but we can understand from their response to this refusal that they would only have hindered the work. Already there were those on the rebuilding team who were discouraging their brothers and sisters in the temple project (see chapter 3). Adding these Samaritans to the team would only have brought more trouble and division. In this offer to help, we can see the attempt of Satan to add more strife among team members.

We need the discernment of the Lord in the work of building the kingdom. Not everyone who comes to us offering assistance is truly called of God. The enemy is quite capable of inspiring his own servants to work with us in the hope that he will create division in the body. Maybe even now in your church, you see evidence of this infiltration of the enemy.

Having been refused positions on the rebuilding team, Israel's adversaries then set out to discourage the people of God. Verse 4 tells us that God's enemies decided to sow seeds of fear among those rebuilding the temple. In verse 5 we find that these enemies hired counselors to work against the building project. These counselors would continue in their attempts to frustrate the Jewish effort from the reign of King Cyrus to the reign of King Darius. Cyrus began his reign in 559 BC, and Darius would begin his reign around 529 BC. This means that for approximately thirty years, these counselors sought to discourage and oppress the Lord's people. Satan does not easily give up.

During the reign of King Xerxes (the Persian name for Ahasuerus, 485-465 BC), these counselors sent a complaint to the king about the people of Judah and Jerusalem (verse

6). Some time later another letter was written to King Artaxerxes of Persia in an attempt to get him to stop the work of rebuilding the temple. This letter is recorded for us in verses 9-16. Notice in verse 10 how those who wrote the letter appeal to their Babylonian heritage. They remind King Artaxerxes that they had been deported and settled in the region of Samaria by Ashurbanipal, the son of King Esharhaddon of Assyria mentioned in verse 2. In mentioning this fact, these Samaritans seem to be reminding the king that they had been sent to Samaria by official decree of the king. This may have been an attempt to gain favor and give credibility to their request.

In their letter the Samaritans informed the king that Jews had returned to Jerusalem to rebuild the city that historically had been evil and rebellious. The Samaritans claimed that if Jerusalem was restored, its inhabitants would no longer pay taxes to the king (verse 13). They told Artaxerxes that they sent him this information because of their allegiance to him (verse 14). They asked that a search of the archives be made to confirm their accusations against Jerusalem.

These enemies knew that if the king did a search, he would find elements of truth in their claim. Babylon and Assyria had been the enemies of Israel. Judah's kings had rebelled against Babylon. We have the record of King Jehoiakim's rebellion against Babylon in 2 Kings 24:1. King Zedekiah also rebelled against Babylon (2 Kings 24:20). God's people did not always accept his will for their lives. Israel had rebelled against God and his discipline in their lives. Satan knows our failures. He will not hesitate to dig them up and use them to his advantage.

On receipt of the letter, a search was done in the archives to determine whether Israel did pose a threat to the king of Persia. This resulted in a response from the king in the form of a letter to the enemies of Israel. This letter informed them that the search had been done, and it was discovered that the people of Israel had revolted in the past. It was also discovered that Jerusalem had powerful kings in the past. As a result King Artaxerxes commanded that the work on the temple and the rebuilding of the city be stopped until further orders (verse 21). Israel's enemies were commissioned by the king to be sure that the rebellious city was not rebuilt so that the Jews could pose a threat to the king of Persia.

As soon as the Samaritan leaders read the letter, they sent word of the king's order to the Jews. Notice in verse 23 that these enemies used force to bring the Lord's work to a halt. The Lord's enemies now had legal rights to stop the rebuilding of the temple and the city of Jerusalem. Throughout the reign of Artaxerxes, the work ceased. It would not be until after his death that another attempt would be made to complete the work.

What we need to see here is the way in which Satan sought to hinder the work of God. It should not surprise us that he is doing the same thing today. He will stop at nothing to hinder the work of God. We have seen how Satan divided the generations in the last chapter. Then he riled Israel's neighbors against them. He was even successful in using the king of Persia, and for a time the work on the temple did stop. It seemed that the enemy had defeated the purpose of God. God's people were divided and discouraged. The enemy was oppressing them. God was not finished with his people, however. He would not give victory to the enemy. Though hindered for a time, God's people would yet see victory.

For Consideration:

• What do we learn here about how the enemy seeks to attack and defeat the purposes of God? Is there evidence of his presence in the work of your church?

- How can the enemy use our past failures in his attempt to defeat us?

- What does this passage teach us about the need for discernment in the work of the kingdom of God?

- What do we learn here about the power of the enemy to bring the work of God to a temporary halt?

For Prayer:

- Ask the Lord to give you greater discernment in the work he has called you to do.

- Ask the Lord to open the eyes and the eyes of the leaders of your church to the ways the enemy is trying to discourage the work of God.

- Thank the Lord that while we have not always lived as we ought to live, he is able to use even our failures to accomplish his purposes. Thank him for the forgiveness he offers.

- Thank the Lord that while the enemy may succeed in halting or hindering the work of God for a time, he cannot have ultimate victory. Thank the Lord that he has already defeated Satan and that our victory is assured.

5

Haggai's Challenge

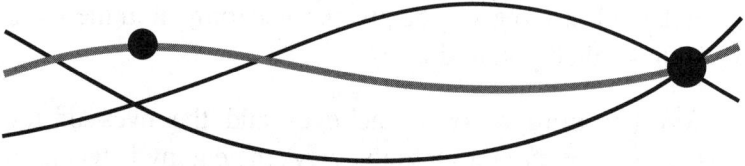

Read Ezra 5:1–17

The work on the temple had ceased. The enemies of God's people had written a letter to the king of Persia who responded by stopping all work of reconstruction. If the enemies had their way, the temple in Jerusalem would never be rebuilt. This order of the king was a setback for the people of God, but they would get back on their feet again.

The prophets Haggai and Zechariah were ministering in the region of Judah at this time. They approached the people of God and challenged them to return to the work of rebuilding the temple, despite the order of the king of Persia.

Scripture does call us to be obedient to the governmental authorities over us. There are times, however, when earthly authorities command us to do something contrary to the will and purpose of God. In this kind of situation, we must learn to obey God and accept the consequences of our actions.

(This was the experience of the apostles in Acts 4:19-20.) In verse 1 the prophets remind the Jews that the Lord God is over them. It was to the Lord that they were to be obedient. It was very clear that the Lord had spoken to King Cyrus of Persia and commanded him to send the Israelites back to their land to rebuild the temple. Haggai and Zechariah challenged the people to obedience. The people needed this challenge at this time in their lives.

The result of this challenge was that Zerubbabel and Jeshua set to work on the house of the Lord. The prophets of God joined them. In making this decision, the leaders were risking their lives. In Ezra 4:23 the work had ceased when their enemies had exercised force to stop them, acting under King Artaxerxes's order. Zerubbabel, Jeshua, and the prophets were willing to take the risk and moved forward, trusting their Lord.

It was not long before Tattenai, the Persian governor of the region, heard about the work. He approached the Israelites about this, asking them by whose authority they were moving ahead with construction. Tattenai demanded to know the names of those who dared to defy the king's order.

This was a difficult moment for the people of God. They did not know what the response of their enemies would be. Notice, however, in verse 5 that "the eye of their God was watching over the elders of the Jews, and they were not stopped." A report of their activities, however, was sent to Darius, the new king of Persia. The encouragement for us is that when we move forward in obedience to the Lord, he watches over us. There will be great risks to take in advancing the Lord's kingdom, but the eye of the Lord is on us and we can rely fully on him. We do not need to be afraid.

The letter sent by Governor Tattenai to King Darius explained what the Jews were doing. In the letter the governor explained how the work of rebuilding the temple was moving ahead. When the Jews were questioned about this work, they informed him that they were following the orders of King Cyrus who had sent them to Israel for this very purpose. Tattenai requested the directions of the new king concerning the situation.

There are several important lessons in this passage. First, we need to see how easy it is for us to be discouraged by the enemy. The work of God was stopped because the enemy succeeded in arousing fear in God's people. This fear kept God's people from obeying the Lord.

Second, notice that there are times when the people of God need to be challenged to return to the Lord and his purposes. Haggai and Zechariah were instruments in the hands of God to bring the Israelites back to the right path. Maybe there are individuals you need to speak to today who have not been obedient to the Lord because of their fear of the enemy or of what might happen if they continued in obedience. Maybe you can be like Haggai or Zechariah to someone today.

Third, obedience to the Lord will not always be easy. The leaders who returned to the construction site were taking a step of faith. They did not know what the response of the enemy would be, but they were willing to take a risk. Not much can be accomplished without risk in the Christian life. Any soldier knows that when he steps on the battlefield, he is taking a risk. Each step we take to conquer enemy territory is a step of faith. We must be ready to face those risks with faith in God.

Finally, notice that the eyes of the Lord were on those who were willing to take the risk and walk in faith. When God saw the way in which the enemy was trying to discourage his people, he held the enemy back so that the Israelites could be obedient. God will do the same for all who will take that step of obedience.

For Consideration:

- Has the enemy ever discouraged you in the Lord's work to the point where you could no longer continue? What is the challenge of this passage for you?

- Are there individuals around you who have been discouraged in their ministries? What would God have you to do or say to them to encourage them to live in obedience?

- How has the enemy been seeking to discourage you in your ministry? What comfort do you find in this passage?

- Is there something that God has called you to do in which you are hesitant? What keeps you from taking the risk and moving forward in faith?

For Prayer:

- Thank the Lord that his eyes are on us to protect and keep us in our service for him.

- Ask the Lord to give you greater faith to take the risks necessary in the ministry to which he has called you.

- Thank the Lord that he is bigger than any enemy that can come against you today.

6

The Temple Is Completed

Read Ezra 6:1–22

Haggai and Zechariah had challenged the people of God to complete the construction of the temple. They did this despite the efforts of their opponents to hinder them. The priests and Levites, in particular, heard the challenge of these two prophets and took the task to heart. This resulted in the adversarial Samaritans writing a letter to the king of Persia, seeking his advice. The hope was that the king would give authority to stop the work.

On receipt of the letter, King Darius issued an order that the archives be searched to see if there ever was a decree permitting the Israelites to rebuild the temple. A scroll was found in the citadel of Ecbatana in the province of Media. In that scroll was the decree of King Cyrus commanding the Jews to rebuild the temple. Cyrus had even given the dimensions of the temple and a general plan the Jews were to follow in its construction. Clearly stated in this decree was that the costs for this construction were to be paid by the royal treasury (see verse 4). The gold and silver articles taken by Nebuchadnezzar from the old temple were also to be returned to Jerusalem.

When King Darius saw the decree, he commanded Tattenai, the governor of the region of the Trans-Euphrates, to refrain from hindering the work on the temple. Darius told the governor not to interfere with the Jews and their work. Darius confirmed the decree of Cyrus and issued an order for the work of the temple reconstruction to be completed.

King Darius also ordered the leaders of the enemies of Israel to help the Jews in this construction. He ordered that the costs for rebuilding the temple be paid out of the royal treasury as Cyrus had previously decreed. Young bulls, rams, and male lambs were to be given to the Jews for burnt offerings to the God of Israel. The enemies of Israel were also to give the Jewish priests daily provisions of wheat, wine, and oil. They were not to fail in this matter so that the Jews in turn would pray to their God for blessings on the king and his sons (see verse 10).

Darius felt so strongly about this decree that he commanded that anyone who failed to obey him in this matter should to be impaled on a beam taken from the perpetrators own house. The house was then to be torn down and destroyed. Darius cursed anyone who might lift a hand to change anything in his decree or hinder in any way the work on the temple in Jerusalem. God had indeed granted his people favor with King Darius, as he had with King Cyrus.

News of this decree encouraged the Jews and they resumed the work on the temple of God. Verse 14 tells us that Haggai and Zechariah preached to the people of Israel during that time. The people received the Word of God warmly and obeyed what they heard. There was renewed enthusiasm and zeal for the work of the temple. God moved in their midst and they saw the victory of the Lord.

It is important that we note here that for quite some time, the people of God were paralyzed by fear in the Lord's work. The foundation had been laid, but the temple remained unfinished. Fear of their enemies had brought a halt to the work. Haggai and Zechariah were used by God to challenge his people to take a risk and move forward in faith and obedience.

The priests and Levites took up that challenge and risked their lives. God blessed that step of faith in a way his people could never have imagined. Not only did the Lord shield his people from their enemies but he also made the enemies pay for the completion of the work. It all began when the priests took the risk and faithfully obeyed the Lord. With that one step of faith, the blessing of God was released on his people.

How often have we found ourselves paralyzed with fear, as were the people of Israel? The work of the kingdom suffers when we fear offending our neighbors more than offending God. Through Haggai and Zechariah, God calls us today. He challenges us to take the risk of obedience, regardless of the circumstance. The Lord shows us in this chapter that we have no cause for fear. Our God is able to do far more than we could ever ask or think. His kingdom expands when we willingly take the risk and step out in faith and obedience.

God moved through the ministries of Haggai and Zechariah, who were preaching in those days. When the temple was completed, God's people held a service of dedication in Jerusalem (verse 16). On that day one hundred bulls, two thousand rams, and four hundred male lambs were sacrificed. They also sacrificed twelve male goats as a sin offering for the twelve tribes of Israel. The priests and Levites were also installed in Jerusalem, according to their family divisions and responsibilities.

On the fourteenth day of the first month, the Passover was celebrated. The priests and Levites purified themselves and slaughtered the Passover lamb. The Israelites separated themselves from their unclean practices and sought the Lord. For seven days after the Passover, they celebrated the Feast of Unleavened Bread by separating themselves from anything with leaven. Leaven or yeast in the Scripture is a symbol of sin. By celebrating this feast, the people of God symbolized their desire to separate themselves from sin in all its forms to serve the Lord, recognizing him as the one who brought them from slavery in Egypt to give them a land of their own. Their hearts were filled with joy because God had caused the king of Persia to favor them.

A responsibility falls on all whom God has blessed. The feast that the Israelites celebrated that day was a reminder that they were a people blessed by God. As they walked in obedience to him and stepped out in faith, God did marvelous things. He opened doors they never thought possible. May we too have the courage to step out in obedient faith. All who willingly take the risk will be surprised at what God will do.

For Consideration:

- What do we learn here about the importance of obeying the Lord in all circumstances?

- What is the promise in this passage for those who willingly step out in faith?

- What is the responsibility of those who have been blessed by God as Israel was in those days?

- Is there anything that God has called you to do that causes you fear? Does this fear keep you from walking in obedience?

For Prayer:

- Ask the Lord to help you to see his purpose for you. Ask him to give you courage to step out in obedience.

- Thank the Lord for the way he cares for us as we move forward in faith.

- Thank the Lord for the blessings he has given you this day. Ask him to help you to live in grateful obedience and thanksgiving.

7

Ezra Comes To Jerusalem

Read Ezra 7:1–28

One of the most confusing things about the study of the kings of Persia is the fact that there are many kings by the same name. Xerxes, Artaxerxes, and Darius were common names among the kings of Persia. Also, sometimes the names of the kings were recorded in the Persian language and sometimes in the Greek language. It is important that we understand this if we are to make sense of what is happening in the book of Ezra.

Verse 1 tells us that it was during the reign of King Artaxerxes of Persia that Ezra left Babylon to go to Jerusalem. This Artaxerxes is not the same Artaxerxes mentioned in chapter 4. The Artaxerxes mentioned here reigned from 465–424 BC.

Verses 1–5 give us the detail of Ezra's family line. The genealogy shows that he was part of a priestly line. He was a man of reputation from a renown family in Israel. It should also be remembered that when the people returned to Israel from exile, the priests had to prove their priesthood by showing their family line. There was no exception for Ezra. His line was confirmed and he was qualified to act in the capacity of priest for God's people in Israel.

Not only did Ezra come from a line of priests but verse 6 shows us that he was also a teacher, well versed in the Law of Moses. He was qualified by means of his line, but he was also qualified because he knew the Word of God. There is another important detail we need to see in verse 6 concerning Ezra. The king had given him everything he had asked for because the hand of the Lord was on him. God's particular anointing was on Ezra to accomplish the work he had called him to do. God equips those he calls.

In the Old Testament period, only certain individuals could become priests. In those days the call of God was on families and family lines. It was for this reason that the family line needed to be established for the priests who returned to Israel. A priest needed to be called of God to exercise his function. In the New Testament period, God calls people to ministry without regard to family lines. However, the call to ministry is still important. While we are all called to be servants of God, he has called some to minister in a full-time capacity or office in the church and others to work in a business or as skilled laborers. It is important for us to know what God has called and gifted us to do so we can walk in obedience to that call.

A calling is not in itself sufficient. Notice that Ezra was well versed in the Law of Moses. In order for this to take place, he had to study the Law and understand its application. Ezra was trained in the truth of the Word of God. You may be called to be a pastor but not ready to exercise that calling because you do not have a good grasp of the truth of the Word of God. While our calling is essential, we also need to be trained in the Word so that we can exercise that calling effectively. How can we lead men and women into the truth of God if we are unfamiliar with that truth ourselves? Ezra was called of God and knew that calling, but he also was trained in the truth of the Word of God.

There is another aspect that we should not miss. Calling and training are essential, but there is something else we need if we are going to have an effective ministry. The hand of the Lord was on Ezra, blessing what he was doing. It is quite possible for us to be called and trained and still not experience the blessing of the Lord on our ministries.

It is all too easy for us to believe that our calling and training are sufficient. Many times, we believe that because we have the training, we can change the world. The reality of the matter is that unless God touches what we do, all our training is in vain. Maybe you have seen God use in a powerful way a simple man or woman who had no training at all. Maybe you have been frustrated because, with all your training, you do not seem to have the impact you would like on those you minister to. Unless the Lord's hand is on our ministries, nothing of any real significance will ever be accomplished. Ezra was called and trained but, more than all this, the hand of the Lord was on him, blessing the ministry to which he had been called.

When Ezra left for Jerusalem, he was accompanied by a team of Israelites. Among them were priests, Levites, singers, gatekeepers, and temple servants. The journey took four months and the hand of the Lord blessed them as they traveled (verse 9). Verse 10 leads us to believe that there was a very special reason why the hand of the Lord was on Ezra. We are told that God's hand was on him because he devoted himself to study so that he could observe and teach the laws of God to Israel. We need to look at this verse in greater detail.

Ezra devoted himself to the study of the Word. To devote oneself to something requires discipline and sacrifice. Ezra was willing to sacrifice other interests for the sake of knowing the Word of God. There are many things that draw our attention away from the Scriptures. Other activities and interests seem to crowd out our time with God. Ezra committed himself to the study of the Word. He took the time and made the necessary sacrifices.

Not only did Ezra devote himself to the study of the Word but he also devoted himself to the observation of that Word. There is a difference between studying the Word and obeying it. There are many who study the Scriptures who do not apply its principles to their lives. Ezra took the Word seriously. When he discovered a truth, he put it into practice. He let the Law of God challenge his ways. He not only knew the truth but also lived it.

Ezra also taught the Law of God in Israel. What he learned and practiced he passed on to others so that they too would know and live in obedience to the Word of God. It is important to note that he first studied and obeyed the Word before teaching others. How can we teach others to live what we ourselves do not live?

It was because of these qualities that the hand of the Lord was on Ezra. Disobedience will keep us from God. Ignorance of his Word will keep us from understanding his purposes. God is always searching for people who will take him seriously. He delights to reveal himself to those who love him and live by his truth.

When Ezra returned to Jerusalem from exile, he returned with a letter from King Artaxerxes. In this letter the king decreed that any Israelite in his kingdom, who so desired, could return to Jerusalem with Ezra. This was the second group that returned to Jerusalem. King Artaxerxes commissioned Ezra to return to Israel to see that its inhabitants were living in accordance with the Law of God (verse 14). This is not to say that the king was sincerely interested in the Lord God of Israel. Likely, it was the king's desire to please and have the favor of all the gods in his dominion. In Ezra 6:3-10 we see that King Cyrus was interested in pleasing the people of Israel so that they would pray to their God for him. Ezra was to take an offering of gold and silver that the king and his advisors had donated freely for the work of God in Jerusalem.

Included in this offering were freewill offerings from different individuals living in Babylon. The king told Ezra to be sure to purchase bulls, rams, and male lambs as well as grain and drink offerings with the donated money (verse 17). Ezra was then to sacrifice these animals as an offering to the God of Israel on behalf of the king and his advisors. The money that remained was to be used at the discretion of the Jewish leaders in accordance with the will of the Lord. If there was further need, Ezra was given permission to draw from the king's treasury whatever was necessary. Beyond this, King Artaxerxes ordered the treasurers in the region of Trans-Euphrates to provide any financial support Ezra needed for the work of God up to 3.5 tons of silver, 600 bushels of wheat (22 kiloliters), 600 gallons of wine (2.2 kiloliters), 600 gallons of olive oil, and an unlimited quantity of salt.

King Artaxerxes commanded that everything be done so that the temple could be completed and God's worship established in Jerusalem. Artaxerxes did not want the wrath of the God of Israel to be against him and his kingdom. God had put fear in the heart of Artaxerxes so that he respected the Lord God of Israel. In verse 24 we see that the king of Persia even decreed that the temple and temple servants be exempt from paying any taxes to the empire.

Ezra was also to appoint magistrates and judges to administer justice in the land of Israel. He was to select those who knew the Law of God and his requirements. Ezra was also commissioned to teach anyone who did not know the Law of God. Whoever did not obey the laws of the God of Israel, according to Artaxerxes, was to be punished by banishment, confiscation of property, imprisonment, or death.

It is quite amazing to see how God so moved in the heart of this pagan Persian king. Ezra praised the Lord as he considered what God was doing that day. God had given Ezra favor in the eyes of the king. We can only pray that we would see this happen in our own land.

Seeing how God had given him such favor, Ezra took courage and set out to accomplish the purpose of God in Jerusalem. God blessed his people as they built the temple. When the temple was completed, he sent Ezra to teach the people of the land the ways of the Lord. It was the purpose of God to establish his people, guide them into true worship, and bless them in his ways.

For Consideration:

• What do we learn in this passage about the importance of calling, training, and anointing for ministry?

• How important is it for us to know the calling, training, and anointing of God on our lives and ministries?

• Why was the hand of God's favor on Ezra?

• How important was the favor of God for Ezra? Where would he have been without the favor of God on his life and ministry?

• What do we learn here about the type of person God uses? Compare Ezra and Artaxerxes. How does God use each of these men?

For Prayer:

• Ask the Lord to help you to be sure of his calling on your life.

- Ask the Lord to give you a deeper burden for his Word.

- Thank the Lord for the way his hand has been on you.

- Ask God to show you anything that keeps you from experiencing his favor on your life and ministry.

8

The Return of the Exiles with Ezra

Read Ezra 8:1–36

We have seen how King Artaxerxes commissioned Ezra to return to the city of Jerusalem to train the people in the Law of God. At that time the king decreed that any Israelite who wanted to return to Jerusalem could do so, and a number of Israelites decided to return to their homeland with Ezra.

The first part of chapter 8 gives us the names of those who went with Ezra to Jerusalem during the reign of King Artaxerxes. Note that each of these individuals is listed according to family. It was important that all people prove their status as Israelites. The task of building the kingdom of God belonged to his people. Those who returned needed to prove that they were the covenant people of God. They were able to demonstrate this by tracing their family lines.

Those who were returning to Jerusalem assembled at a canal that flowed toward the Ahava River. They camped there for three days while Ezra checked to see who was among them. Ezra discovered that there were no Levites in the group. The Levites had the responsibility of ministering in the temple, and Ezra did not want to return without these temple workers.

The king had commissioned Ezra to instruct God's people in his Law. To do this Ezra needed help of the Levites. It is uncertain why there were no Levites among those returning that day, but Ezra had enough discernment to recognize this as a problem. He called some of the key leaders together and sent them to a man by the name of Iddo who was in charge of a group of temple servants in the region of Casiphia (verse 17). Iddo was able to persuade a number of Levites to return with Ezra to Jerusalem.

It is important to note that while Iddo was influential in these Levites joining Ezra's group, Ezra gave the credit to the Lord God. In verse 18 he clearly states that it was because of the gracious hand of the Lord God on them that these Levites joined them. We make the effort, but none of our efforts will succeed without the hand of the Lord God moving on our behalf. In total 38 Levites agreed to return to Jerusalem. Another 220 temple servants commissioned to help the Levites also agreed to join the returning exiles. All of these individuals were registered by name and joined the group camped by the Ahava Canal.

How easy it would have been to overlook the absence of Levites and temple servants in that group of returning exiles. Ezra was returning to guide God's people in obedience to the Law, and he could not have done this by himself. These Levites and temple helpers were very important in the fulfillment of his task. Ezra understood the importance of a team to accomplish the work of God. We need each other if the work of God is going to advance. Ezra made it a priority to see that the team was complete before going on his mission.

Now that Ezra was assured that he had the people necessary for the task, he gathered them together and proclaimed a fast to humble themselves before God and ask for a safe journey. This fast reminded the people of God that the success or failure of their journey did not depend on themselves but on God. It would have been easy for the Israelites to attempt this journey in their own wisdom and skill. By proclaiming this fast, Ezra was reminding the returning exiles of the source of their strength and wisdom. He set their minds on the Lord God as the protector and source of strength for the journey. It would do us all well to take the time before each of our endeavors to remind ourselves that it is only in the strength of the Lord that we can do anything of lasting value.

Ezra did not want to ask the king for soldiers and horsemen to protect them on the way to Jerusalem. He told the king that the hand of the Lord God was on those who looked to him, and Ezra wanted to demonstrate this to the king by trusting the Lord God alone for protection during the journey. Also, Ezra wanted the Israelites to experience the reality of God's care and provision as they journeyed. It would have been easy to lean on the good favor of the king for security, but Ezra chose to rely on God alone.

We need to understand that while Ezra would not have sinned by asking the king for soldiers and horsemen to join him on the trip, he had a leading from the Lord to refuse this offer (verse 23). God wanted to teach his people an important lesson of trust and this was the means of teaching that lesson.

God must be our trust. It is true that the Lord will use others to accomplish his purposes in our lives, but our dependence must remain on God alone. Ezra had this kind of confidence in God. That day the gathered Jews fasted and prayed to the Lord, and he heard their prayer and blessed their journey.

In verse 24 notice how Ezra dealt with the financial provisions that had been given to him for the temple in Jerusalem. He set apart twelve of the leading priests and ten others. He weighed out the offerings of silver and gold and the other articles. This group of people together weighed out 650 talents of silver (over 25 tons), 100 talents of silver articles (approximately 4 tons), 100 talents of gold, 20 gold bowls with a value of 1,000 darics (approximately 20 pounds), and fine articles of polished bronze. All these articles were weighed in the presence of witnesses. Ezra reminded these individuals that they and these articles had been consecrated to God. In reminding them of this consecration, Ezra was calling them to integrity. He reminded them that God would hold them accountable for these articles. Ezra challenged them to guard the articles carefully until they were weighed again in the house of the Lord (verse 29).

Ezra expected absolute honesty from these men, but he also did all he could to hold them accountable. He weighed everything and recorded the weight. These priests were expected to hand over to the temple that same amount at the end of the journey in the presences of the priests and Levites of the temple. Ezra trusted these priests, but he did not put a stumbling block before them. We all are tempted to sin. It is for this reason that we do our best to keep from going places where we know we will be tempted. For the good of the body of Christ, we may need to put similar safeguards in place to avoid any confusion or opportunity for the enemy to cause suspicion. When these leaders arrived in Jerusalem and presented the exact amount of gold and silver to the priests at the temple, no one could even wonder if they had kept any for themselves.

Now that everything was in place, Ezra and those who went with him left for Jerusalem. They left on the twelfth day of the first month. God protected them from enemies and bandits on the way. Upon arrival they took three days to rest. On the fourth day, they went to the temple and weighed out the silver and gold that had been given to them. All these articles were handed over to the priests and Levites in the temple as a gift from the king of Persia and the remaining Israelites in the region of Babylon. After verifying that nothing was missing, the weight was again recorded.

When these treasures were handed over, the exiles who had returned from captivity with Ezra brought burnt offerings to the Lord God. They sacrificed twelve bulls, one for each tribe. Also sacrificed that day were ninety-six rams, seventy-seven male lambs, and twelve male goats as a sin offering. This was in accordance with the command of King Artaxerxes. The king's orders were given to the governor, commanding him to give from his treasury all that was necessary for the work of the Lord.

As we look at Ezra's journey, several things stand out. Ezra was a man of tremendous discernment. He carefully considered the will and purpose of God in what he did. This led him to recognize that there were no Levites in the group that had gathered to return. He also recognized his need of God for a safe journey. He did not trust in his own strength and wisdom; instead, he relied fully on God. Ezra demanded absolute honesty and integrity from those who served with him and sought ways to hold them accountable before God and each other. He provided no opening for the enemy to enter. These are all valuable lessons we can learn from his example.

For Consideration:

- Why was it important that Ezra have Levites on his journey to Jerusalem? What things might we overlook in the work of the church in our day?

- How did Ezra find a balance between relying on God and enlisting the services of men of faith in order to find Levites?

- Can we trust people and still demand that they give an account of what they are doing? Does the fact that Ezra required a weighing of the gold and silver mean that he did not trust his men? How important is accountability, especially in financial matters?

- What evidence is there that the confidence of Ezra was in the Lord God? Have you ever found yourself relying on someone or something else? Explain.

For Prayer:

- Ask the Lord to help you to be absolutely honest and accountable to others.

- Thank the Lord that he promises to be with you and to guide you in all things. Ask him to forgive you for the times you have not always trusted him.

- Ask the Lord to open your eyes to see how his hand has been on you. Take a moment to praise him for his blessings.

9

The Sins of the People

Read Ezra 9:1–15

E zra and the group that had come with him from exile had arrived in the city of Jerusalem. It was not long before Ezra discovered that there were real problems in Israel. Already the people of God had fallen into sin.

From verse 1 we discover that the people had not kept themselves separate from the neighboring people. In other words, Israelites had intermarried with unbelievers around them. Verse 2 makes it very clear that they had "mingled the holy race with the peoples around them." The leaders in particular were leading the way in this practice. In addition, the returning Jews had begun to take on the ungodly practices of the unbelievers. The Jews were not remaining true to the Lord God and his Word. Even the priests were guilty in this regard.

It was God's desire that his people be pure before him. In Deuteronomy 7:1–4 the Lord told his people that he did not want them to give their sons and daughters to the foreigners around them. These foreigners did not belong to the Lord. Their practices were contrary to the purposes of God and would lead God's people away from him. It was for this reason that the Lord commanded his people to marry only among themselves. God's people, guided by their spiritual and political leaders, had chosen to disobey this clear command of God. They took foreign husbands and wives. These unbelieving spouses led the returned exiles to wander from the principles of God's Word. The Israelites even began to once again adopt foreign, evil practices.

It is the desire of God that we give ourselves entirely to him. He wants us for himself. Nothing must stand between the Lord and us. We must jealously guard our relationship with him. We must live and be seen as the people of God. All practices that do not agree with the clear teachings of Scripture must be abandoned.

On hearing about these intermarriages, Ezra tore his tunic and cloak. In his grief he tore hair from his head and beard. He sat appalled at such evil in the land. We can only admire a man like this. Ezra took the Word of God seriously. He was grieved when the Lord's commands were disregarded. His heart broke because his people had turned their backs on God. The Israelites of that day did not have a burden for the Word of God. They had become lax in their faith.

We need to see more people like Ezra in our day. Do we grieve when we see the people of God falling into sin and abandoning the truth of Scripture? Ezra was a man whose heart was in tune with the heart of God.

Ezra was not alone that day. There were others in the land that joined him in his grief until the evening sacrifice (verse 4). Together they sat in sickened anguish. What could they say? They likely waited on the Lord for guidance and direction. When the time for the evening sacrifice came, Ezra fell to his knees with torn clothes. He spread his hands out to the Lord God in prayer and confession. His prayer reflected something of his heart.

Ezra cried out to God, saying that he was too ashamed and disgraced to lift up his face because of the sins of his people. We need to remember that Ezra was not guilty himself, but he was ashamed for the sins of his people. God burdened his heart with the weight of the sin around him. God was using Ezra to intercede for his people. Those called to intercede often experience a deep burden in prayer. True intercession is often difficult. In order to enable his intercessors to pray more effectively, God may place a heavy burden on their hearts. This seems to be what happened to Ezra. He felt the grief of God over sin in the land. Ezra cried out from a heart that was deeply moved.

Ezra recognized that the guilt of God's people went back in time. From the days of their ancestors until that day, God's people had strayed from the truth of his Word. God had often judged Israel for her sins. The Lord had sent enemies to punish his guilty people with the sword. The Lord had given Israel's land to her enemies and sent her into captivity. Israel's enemies had pillaged the land and humiliated her at the hands of foreign kings. Despite all this, God's people still wandered from him. Their hearts remained wicked and unchanged.

In verse 8 Ezra recognizes that it was only by God's grace that his people had returned to the land of Israel. It was because of the gracious hand of God that they had completed the temple and had been released from their bondage in Babylon. Notice, however, in verse 8 that it was "for a brief moment" that God had been gracious. In saying this Ezra recognized that just as God had stripped his blessings from their ancestors because of sin, so he could do the same to them. Ezra did not take the graciousness of God for granted.

How important it is for us to understand this in our day as well. We can begin to feel secure in the blessings of God. Sometimes we may even begin to feel that God owes us these blessings. What we need to understand is that God can strip these from us in an instant.

At that moment Israel was experiencing the wonderful hand of a gracious God. He had rescued his people from the captivity of the kings of Persia (verse 9). The Lord had remembered his people and set them free for a purpose. It was his desire that his people honor him. He wanted to restore them to their former glory and through them spread the light of his truth. He was enabling them to repair what their sin had destroyed. He had surrounded them with his protection and kept their enemies from harming them. The Israelites were a people of purpose. They had been called of God to be his instruments in the world. What a privilege was theirs as his chosen children.

God's people, however, had failed him again. Despite his wonderful purpose, they had turned their backs on him. They chose to disregard his commands and wandered into error. In particular, we see in this chapter that God's people had disregarded his command not to marry the foreign unbelievers in the neighboring lands. These disobedient Jews had corrupted their testimony and covered their light. God had commanded them not to marry foreign, ungodly spouses. Not only had they done so, they had also adopted pagan practices. They were behaving the same as their evil neighbors. The glory of God was no longer in their midst.

In the past the Israelites had brought the wrath of God on themselves by their rebellious hearts. Ezra reminds his people in verse 13 that while God had punished them for their evil, their punishment had been less than their sin deserved. God had been gracious to his rebellious people and had not completely destroyed them.

Ezra understood that God was under no obligation to spare his people. God had often tried to reach his people through the prophets and priests of the day, but the Israelites had continually refused to listen. God had the right to condemn his sinful people for all eternity because of his holiness. His people had never fully appreciated his deep and intense hatred for sin. They had failed to understand just how serious a situation they were in.

The sin of God's people had sent them into exile in the first place. When, by God's grace, his people had been able to return to Jerusalem, it was not long before they were again blinded to the reality of sin and its effect on their life as a nation. May God open our eyes to the reality of sin and its horrible nature.

For Consideration:

- God's people had become blind to their own spiritual condition. To what extent have we become blind in our day to the seriousness of sin in our midst?

- Through Ezra we are reminded that God was seeking a holy race to be a light in this world. Have you been faithful? Do people see righteousness in your life?

- What do we learn here about the gift of intercession? Have you ever felt an intense burden to pray for something or for someone?

- How seriously do we take sin in our day?

- Has the church of our day been guilty of compromising the faith? What worldly influences do we see in the church today?

For Prayer:

- Ask the Lord to open your eyes to the seriousness of sin.

- Ask the Lord to open your heart to the truth of his Word. Ask him to enable you to apply that truth in your daily life.

- Ask God to search your heart and reveal to you any sin or area of rebellion. Confess this sin and make things right with God.

- Ask the Lord to move in your life, in the life of your church, and in the life of your nation to bring conviction of sin.

10

Restoration

Read Ezra 10:1–44

E zra confessed the sins of his people. His heart was broken by the fact that these Israelites, who had returned from exile, had so quickly turned from the Lord their God. They had married foreign spouses and adopted their evil practices. Before God and the congregation of Israel, Ezra confessed the sins of his people and sought the will of God in how to make things right.

Notice in verse 1 the extent of Ezra's grief. He wept and threw himself down to the ground before the house of the Lord. He did this in the presence of Israel. His actions drew men and women of like mind until a large crowd had gathered around him. Together they wept and grieved over their sins as God stirred the hearts of his people. This humility was necessary if his people were to be restored. We need to understand the seriousness of our sin before we can see our need for a cure. Before moving in power to restore and renew his people, God will often begin by bringing a deep awareness and conviction of sin. It is one thing to grieve over sin; it is another to do something about that sin. It was a man by the name of Shecaniah who shifted the focus from grief and mourning to making things right. It is as though Ezra had been so caught up in the grief of the moment that he was unable to move beyond that grief to doing something about the evil in the land. God used Shecaniah to move to the next stage.

Shecaniah agreed that the men of Judah had been unfaithful in marrying foreign women. He reminded them, however, that this was not the end of the nation. There was still hope. Shecaniah recognized that God is a gracious God, full of compassion. Though the people's sin was great, God had not forsaken them.

We need to find a balance between grieving over our sin and recognizing the grace of our Lord to forgive. It is all too easy in our preaching to emphasize human sinfulness and neglect the grace and compassion of Christ. On the other hand, it is also easy to emphasize the forgiveness and compassion of Christ and fail to teach others how serious sin really is. It is important for us to maintain a healthy balance between the awfulness of sin and the grace and forgiveness of God. At this point Ezra and the nation had not moved beyond the stage of grieving over sin.

Shecaniah proposed a solution. He suggested that Israel make a covenant before the Lord to send away all foreign women and children, according to the Law of the Lord. He challenged Ezra and the people to take courage, to rise, and make things right. This was exactly what God's people needed. They were grieving over their sin, but no one was thinking about making things right with God. The enemy does not fear confession so much as he fears those who rise to make things right.

There have been many times in my life when I was not able to move past the confession of my sin. I confessed my sins before God but failed to accept his grace and forgiveness. Satan loves to see Christians remain in a sense of defeat. He takes great delight in reminding us of how sinful we are. He wants us to remain in that sense of sinfulness and defeat. As long as we live as though we are defeated, we are no threat to Satan. He fears those, however, who realize their sin and then rise to do something about it. This was the challenge of Shecaniah.

No matter what your sin has been, there is still hope. Don't let Satan tell you that you are forever defeated. Don't let him keep you down. Confess your sin. Take courage and do something about it. Make things right between you and God.

Ezra heard the challenge of Shecaniah and listened to his counsel. The time of confession was over. The time had come to do something about the problem. Ezra put the priests, Levites, and all of Israel under oath to do what Shecaniah had suggested. That day they took an oath to do whatever was necessary to correct the situation and be restored to a right relationship with God.

Having taken this step, Ezra then withdrew from the house of the Lord. He found a room where he could find some privacy and continued to mourn and grieve before God. During that time he fasted and sought the Lord. While Ezra understood the grace and compassion of God, he had been called to pray. His burden for the people of Israel would not be taken from him until they were in a right relationship with God. The Lord's call on him for that moment was to pray. God had called others to act, but Ezra was to continue seeking the face of God. No doubt, during that time Ezra prayed that God would move in the hearts of his people and guide the priests and Levites. This was Ezra's role.

As Ezra prayed, a proclamation was issued throughout Jerusalem and Judah for all the exiles to gather in Jerusalem. Any man who failed to appear within three days would lose his property and be banished from the land. It should be remembered that Ezra had the authority of the king to punish anyone who did not follow the Law of the Lord (Ezra 7:25–26).

Within three days all the men of Israel came to Jerusalem. As they gathered in the square before the temple of the Lord, the rain fell. The people were uncomfortable, cold, and wet as they waited to hear what Ezra had to tell them (verse 9). Ezra stood up that day and told the men that they had been unfaithful in marrying foreign women. He called them to separate from their foreign wives and be restored to God. The Lord moved in power that day, and the assembly was convicted of their sin. With one voice they agreed to separate from their foreign wives. Ezra was seeing the answer to his prayers.

It was decided that this matter could not be dealt with in one day. The assembled people agreed that each man who had married a foreign woman would come at a set time before the elders and judges of the land and deal with this matter. Only a few men opposed the idea.

Ezra selected family heads from each division of Israel to meet with him. Together they sat down to investigate each case. At the end of three months, the leaders of Israel had dealt with all the men who had married foreign women. In verses 18-43 we have a list of men who had married foreigners. Each case was decided individually and appropriate sacrifices were made for their sin.

Not only were the foreign women to be sent away but so were the children who had been born through these women (verse 44). This would not be easy for these families. Being restored to a right relationship with God meant sacrifice for these individuals and their families. There are times when

God will call us to sacrifice our loved ones for his cause. Jesus makes it quite clear in the Gospel of Matthew that he must take priority even over our families: "Anyone who loves his father or mother more than me is not worthy of me; anyone who loves his son or daughter more than me is not worthy of me." (Matthew 10:37).

The call to seek God with all our hearts goes out today as well as it did in the days of Ezra. Ezra challenged his people to make things right with God, no matter the cost. This will not always be easy, but it will always bring blessing.

For Consideration:

- What do we learn here about the balance between confession and making things right?

- What role did prayer and intercession play in this restoration of God's people?

- Ezra and Shecaniah seem to have had different roles. How important is it for us to understand our role in the body of Christ?

- What do we learn here about the cost of restoration? How much would you be willing to give up to be restored to a right relationship with God?

- What stands between you and God today?

For Prayer:

- Ask God to search your heart and reveal to you any sin that keeps you from a deeper relationship with him.

- Ask the Lord to give you the willingness to sacrifice whatever it takes to be restored to him.

- Ask the Lord to help you understand your role in enabling God's people to be restored to him.

Nehemiah

11

Nehemiah's Prayer

Read Nehemiah 1:1–11

Nehemiah lived in the days of Ezra when the people of God were returning from exile in Babylon to rebuild the city of Jerusalem. When this book begins, Nehemiah is in the citadel of Susa, the winter residence of the Persian kings. Nehemiah was an important servant of the reigning king of Persia. God had sovereignly placed Nehemiah in this position as an instrument to accomplish the Lord's purposes in Jerusalem.

When Nehemiah was in Susa, one of his Jewish brothers came to see him. This brother, by the name of Hanani, had just returned from Judah. Nehemiah questioned him about the Jews who had survived the exile and returned to Jerusalem. Hanani told Nehemiah that these individuals were in great trouble and disgrace. Jerusalem's wall and burned gates still lay in ruin. The exiles were living in poor conditions. God's people had at one time enjoyed wonderful, divine blessing on their land. They had been admired and respected by all the nations of the earth. But things had changed—Jerusalem was in ruins. As Nehemiah reflected on this, his heart was broken. The picture of his people in disgrace and poverty was more than he could bear. That day God placed a heavy burden on his heart.

Verse 4 tells us that for days Nehemiah could not get the picture of Jerusalem out of his mind. He wept, mourned, and fasted during this time. He "prayed before the God of heaven," the God of Jerusalem. It was the Lord himself who had put this deep burden on Nehemiah's heart because the Lord wanted to use him to accomplish a great purpose for his kingdom. Where there is no burden on the heart of the servant of God, the ministry to which he or she is called will suffer. God was preparing Nehemiah for ministry by placing that burden on his heart.

Verses 5-11 record Nehemiah's prayer for his people. This prayer can be divided into three parts: praise, confession, and petition. We will examine each part separately.

Praise (verse 5)

Nehemiah's prayer begins with praise to God. It is important for us to remember that the reason Nehemiah's heart had been burdened was because of the conditions under which his people were living in Jerusalem. God had punished Israel for rebellion. He had allowed the enemy to invade the land and take the Israelites into captivity. He had allowed the enemy to destroy the temple, break down the wall of Jerusalem, and burn to the ground all the significant buildings.

Although it is not easy to praise the Lord in trials and difficulties, Nehemiah praised the Lord as the great and awesome God of heaven. Surely, Nehemiah did not always understand how God worked. It would not have been easy for Nehemiah to recognize God as great and awesome when everything Nehemiah cherished had been stripped away and lay in a burned pile of rubble. Nehemiah accepted by faith what he knew to be true but could not presently see. He recognized the Lord as an awesome God whose ways are beyond understanding.

Notice also in verse 5 that Nehemiah praised a God "who keeps his covenant of love." Remember the context of this prayer. It would have seemed that the Mosaic covenant had been broken. To the human eye, the Israelites had broken that covenant and God had turned his back on his people. Despite what Nehemiah saw around him, he still believed that God would keep his part of the covenant with his people. Nehemiah believed the promises of God.

Nehemiah was not discouraged by what he saw around him. He trusted God for the impossible. In a time when his human vision was clouded, Nehemiah clung to the promises and clear truth of the Word of God. He had reason to praise the Lord. Though he could not see victory, Nehemiah praised God for it by faith because he trusted God's character.

Confession (verses 6–7)

Having taken the time to praise the Lord, Nehemiah next turns his attention to confessing the sins of his people. He realized that the sins of Israel and Judah had brought these trials on his people. Nehemiah pleaded with God to listen to his prayer for his people, even through they were guilty. In saying this, Nehemiah recognized that God has tremendous compassion, forgiveness, and mercy. Though the sins of his people were terrible, Nehemiah believed that the compassion and grace of his God were even greater. Notice in verse 6 how Nehemiah includes himself as one of those who had rebelled against the Lord God.

In verse 7 Nehemiah spells out the sins of his people. They had acted in a wicked way toward God. They had not obeyed his commands and laws. They had turned their hearts away from God and broken their covenant with him.

Nehemiah accepted the punishment God had placed on his people. Nehemiah recognized that what they had received from the hand of God had been deserved. God had not been unjust. If anything, the Lord had shown great compassion by not completely destroying them as a people. Nehemiah confessed his guilt and the guilt of all Israel and accepted the Lord's punishment.

Petition (verses 8–11)

Some believers never seem to move beyond their guilt. They seem to live their lives believing that their destiny is to live outside the blessings of God because they are unworthy of anything else. While Nehemiah realized that he and his people deserved the wrath and punishment of God, he did not stop there.

In verses 8 and 9, Nehemiah reminds God of the words he had spoken to Moses. God had told Moses that if his people were unfaithful, then he would scatter them among the nations (see Leviticus 26:13–33). God had also promised, however, that if his people obeyed his commands, then even if they were exiled to the farthest corner of the earth, he would gather them together and bring them back to the land he had chosen for them. We can see this promise of God to Moses in Deuteronomy 30:2–5.

Nehemiah did not remain in a posture of defeat and claimed the promise of God to restore the Israelites if they would return to him. Nehemiah reminded God that they were his chosen people. He pleaded with God to hear his prayer for his people. Nehemiah believed it was time for God to move again among his people and restore them to himself.

Verse 11 shows us something else about Nehemiah. Not only had God stirred his heart, he had also moved him to be willing to do something about the situation in Jerusalem. In verse 11 Nehemiah prays that God will give him favor in the eyes of the king. As the cupbearer of the king, Nehemiah had frequent access to the king's presence. We are not told what Nehemiah thought he needed to do, but we can be sure that God had been challenging his heart to be available as the answer to his own prayer.

What we need to see is that when God places a burden on our hearts to pray, he may also call us to do something about that burden. It is relatively easy to pray, but it takes a greater sacrifice to be willing to step out and do something. Nehemiah was willing to do whatever God called him to do. He committed this to the Lord and waited on his direction.

For Consideration:

* What trials are you facing today? Can you praise the Lord in those trials?

* Can there ever be real victory if we do not accept what God has brought our way with praise and thanksgiving? How will bitterness and anger toward God hinder us in our spiritual walk?

* What do we learn here about the compassion and grace of God?

* Is it the will of God that we live in defeat and a constant sense of guilt? What does Nehemiah have to teach us about this?

* What is the connection between the burden to pray and the willingness to step out?

For Prayer:

* Take a moment to recognize that God is sovereign over the trials you are facing right now. Thank him that he will use these trials to accomplish his purpose in your life.

- Thank the Lord that despite our sin and rebellion there is still victory in him.

- Ask the Lord to make you willing to be available to do whatever he would lead you to do for the sake of the burdens he has placed on your heart.

12

Nehemiah's Request

Read Nehemiah 2:1–20

Nehemiah's heart was burdened with the need of his people in the land of Israel. In the last chapter, he cried out to God to do something about that need. He made himself available to the Lord and asked that God would open the heart of the king to grant favor to his people.

We read in Nehemiah 1:1 that it was in the month of Kislev in the twentieth year of Artaxerxes that Nehemiah heard the news of Israel's disgrace. The month of Kislev was the ninth month of the Jewish year. According to Nehemiah 2:1, it was not until the month of Nisan that Nehemiah appeared before the king. Nisan was the first month of the Jewish calendar. This meant that Nehemiah waited about four months before he saw the answer to his prayer.

Though it had been several months since Nehemiah had heard the news from Israel, the burden continued to weigh heavily on his heart. When he appeared before the king, he was feeling depressed. The king took note of his mood and asked him why he was so sad when he was obviously not ill.

This question filled Nehemiah with fear. He does not tell us why he was afraid. We are left to guess. Could it be that it was because the time had come for him to approach the king and speak his heart? Deep down, Nehemiah knew that something needed to be done for his people. Who was he to approach the great king of Persia, one of the most powerful men on the earth, to ask him to do something for the Jews? Though Nehemiah was very much afraid, he told the king that he grieved because the city of his ancestors lay in ruins with the gates destroyed by fire.

Nehemiah had spoken his heart. The king then asked, "What is it you want?" (verse 4). Nehemiah immediately prayed to the Lord. The prayer could not have lasted very long because the king awaited his response. Nehemiah needed wisdom and boldness in his request. More than anything else, however, he needed the Lord to soften the heart of the king so that he would be responsive to the request.

Having committed this matter to the Lord, Nehemiah asked that the king grant him leave from his responsibilities to return to Judah to rebuild the city of Jerusalem. This was a bold request for a cupbearer to make. In verse 6 the king asked Nehemiah how long it would take him to accomplish this goal and when he would be back to his responsibilities. Nehemiah set a time, and it pleased the king to send him.

We can only imagine what Nehemiah felt that day as he watched the Lord God answer his prayers. The spiritual battle had already been won during the four months of prayer. Nehemiah was simply harvesting the fruit of that prayer.

Encouraged by the response of the king, Nehemiah asked even more from King Artaxerxes. In verse 7 he asked him for letters of safe conduct. He also asked for a letter to Asaph, the keeper of the king's forest, to obtain lumber to make beams for the gates of the citadel by the temple, the city wall, and for his own residence. The king again granted his request.

Nehemiah understood that the hand of the Lord was on him for this ministry and that was the reason Artaxerxes was responding so favorably (verse 8). God was opening doors for the restoration of the city of Jerusalem. Nehemiah did not take the credit himself; he gave all the glory to God. How easy it is for us to fall into the trap of believing that somehow because we have had success where others have failed, then we must have special skills and abilities. Nehemiah credited God for the success. This is a lesson we all need to learn.

When Nehemiah was ready to return to Jerusalem, the king sent him with letters to the governors through whose territory he would have to pass so that they would give him safe passage. Also accompanying Nehemiah was a small band of soldiers and cavalry to protect him on the way.

When Ezra had returned to Jerusalem, he had chosen not to use the king's army so that the king would see that God was able to protect his own (Ezra 8:22). Nehemiah, however, accepted the king's escort. Both men did what they thought was right. Nehemiah did not sin by accepting the king's escort. What we need to understand here is that God works with each of us in a different way. His purpose for one person is not the same as his purpose for another. We need to be careful not to judge each other. Instead, we need to accept how God works differently in each person.

When Nehemiah arrived in the region of Judah, two men in particular (Sanballat and Tobiah) were quite disturbed that he had returned to rebuild Jerusalem. These men would prove to be fierce enemies of the work of God as Nehemiah sought to restore the city.

After three days in the city of Jerusalem, Nehemiah set out during the night with a few men. This small group silently went through the city, examining the wall. They told no one of their plans. Even the officials who were governing the land did not know what Nehemiah was doing. Had they known, they would have very likely caused trouble and tried to hinder him in his progress.

The day came, however, when it was time for Nehemiah to share his burden with the people of Israel. In verse 17 Nehemiah addresses the people. He points out how the once glorious city now lay in ruins. He reminds them that they, who were once a glorious people, were living in disgrace. He challenges them to stand up with him and set to work to rebuild the wall of Jerusalem. He also tells them of how the hand of the Lord has been on him, granting him favor in the eyes of King Artaxerxes. Encouraged by this news, the people respond positively: "'Let us start rebuilding.' So they began this good work" (verse 18).

There is something quite sad in these verses that needs to be noted. At that time in the city of Jerusalem, the people of God were living in ruins. They had become content to live in this situation. The wall was broken down. Piles of rubble that once belonged to glorious structures littered the streets, but God's people did nothing. Only when Nehemiah came did they take courage and begin the process of rebuilding. What is sad about this picture is that, for the most part, the people of Israel had begun to accept this as normal. They felt helpless and overwhelmed as many of us in our day. The questions we need to ask ourselves are these: How far from reality is this picture today? Have we, as the people of God, become complacent? Have we allowed the enemy to destroy what God has given us? Christian marriages and families sometimes lie in ruins. The wall of truth is being eroded as God's people allow more and more of the world to influence them. Pillars of morality begin to lean and topple over as one Christian leader after another falls into sin.

Nehemiah challenged his people to take a stand. He showed them that things did not have to be this way. Things could be different. They could rebuild the wall. The pillars could be put in place again. One stone at a time and the work would be done.

The news of the rebuilding of the wall of Jerusalem did not please Judah's neighbors. They did not want to see Israel return to her former glory. As long as God's people lived with a sense of defeat, they were no threat. But when God's people began to realize that victory could be theirs, the enemy began to fear. Satan delights to have us live in defeat and discouragement. As long as we are down, we pose no threat to him. The reality of the matter, however, is that in the Lord Jesus we are able to conquer any enemy that comes our way. We do not have to be defeated by the enemy.

When God's enemies saw that the work of rebuilding the wall had begun, they tried to discourage the workers by mocking and ridiculing them. These enemies even charged the Jews with rebelling against the king. But Nehemiah was not discouraged by the words of his enemies. He reminded them that in the strength of the Lord, God's people would have victory and that the wall would be built. The enemies of God's people would have no part in Jerusalem. They would be driven out and this land would be claimed again for the Lord.

What territory has the enemy taken from you today? Maybe there are individuals who read this commentary who have experienced broken relationships with their brothers or sisters in Christ. Maybe you have failed as a husband or wife. Maybe you have fallen into a particular sin and damaged your testimony for the Lord. Could it be that there is someone reading this commentary who is living in a sense of defeat, as were the children of Israel? Nehemiah's challenge to us today is to rise up and rebuild the walls. He challenges us to straighten out those toppling pillars. He challenges us to reclaim the territory the enemy has taken from us. May God stir up our hearts as he did the hearts of Israel that day to rise and claim the territory we have lost to the enemy. In Christ we can be victorious.

For Consideration:

- What do we learn here about the importance of prayer? How important was prayer in the life of Nehemiah?

- What do we learn here about the difference between Ezra and Nehemiah? What does this teach us about dealing with differences between believers?

- God's people were living in a sense of defeat. Have you ever found yourself in this situation? What can you learn here about God's purpose for victory?

- What walls have been broken down in our faith today?

For Prayer:

- Prayer gave Nehemiah the victory. Ask God to help you to understand the importance of prayer in your ministry and walk with God.

- What territory has the enemy taken from you today? Take a moment to seek the Lord about this. Ask him to restore to you what the enemy has taken.

- Ask God to rebuild his church today to make it everything he intended it to be.

- Ask God to give you a heart to live in victory. Thank him that this victory is ours in him.

13

The Repairs Begin

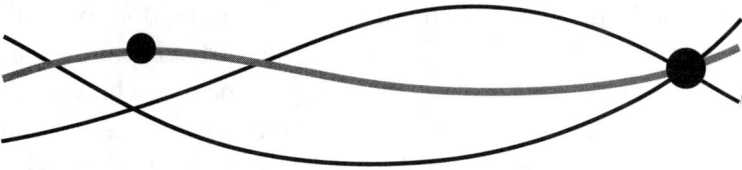

Read Nehemiah 3:1–32

Nehemiah had encouraged the people of God living in Jerusalem to press on and repair the broken wall of the city. This effort required teamwork. In chapter 3 we see the work divided by family. Nehemiah records in this chapter the names of those who worked on the various sections of the wall.

Elishib, the high priest, and his fellow priests took the responsibility of rebuilding the Sheep Gate (verse 1). These priests did not think this work was beneath them. They joyfully took on the task, setting an example for others to follow. The Sheep Gate was the gate through which the sacrifices were brought into the city. It is significant that the priests repaired this gate. Upon completing this task, the priests dedicated this gate and its doors were set in place.

The work of rebuilding the wall was not without its difficulties. In verse 5 we read about the section of the wall repaired by the men of Tekoa. There were nobles among the men of Tekoa who refused to "put their shoulders to the work under their supervisors." We get the impression that these nobles believed that they should have been in charge. They thought that they were too dignified for this kind of work.

There have been times in my personal ministry when God has asked me to do things I did not really want to do. There are times when God will use certain tasks to teach us lessons or to humble us and prepare us for further service. The pride of these nobles only hindered the work of rebuilding the wall. In the work of the kingdom of God, we ought never to be afraid of getting dirty or putting our shoulders to the task. God is looking for people who will do whatever he calls them to do. He is looking for people who will put aside what they think of themselves and set their hearts to whatever service he calls them. There is no rank in the family of God—we are all kings and priests.

In the work of the kingdom of God, there will always be struggle and difficulty. Notice here, however, that the work did not stop because of these arrogant nobles. God used others to accomplish what these men refused to do. Other men were more than willing to lend a hand. In verse 8 we meet a goldsmith and a perfume-maker who offered their services. Realize that as goldsmiths and perfume-makers, they were not necessarily skilled in the hard and heavy work that was required for building the wall. However, they did not allow this to stop them. Although this was not the area of their greatest gifting, it was the work that needed to be done. God will sometimes stretch us in our ministries. He will sometimes ask us to step out into unknown territory. These men were willing to be stretched. We need more people like them today.

Some women also got involved in the construction. In verse 12 we meet a man by the name of Shallum who repaired a certain section of the wall with the help of his daughters. While the nobles of Tekoa stood on the sidelines, arrogantly refusing to help, the daughters of Shallum got on with the task at hand. The spiritual reward of these women would be far greater than that of the nobles of Tekoa. In God's eyes, status and rank in society mean nothing. We are all equal before him.

It is interesting to note in verse 27 that the nobles who refused to work did not discourage the other men of Tekoa who repaired a second section of the wall. While these other men had reason to be discouraged, God gave them grace not only to do their part but even more. Maybe you are in a similar situation. There are those around you who refuse to do their part. Don't let this hinder you in doing what God is calling you to do. Let the Lord God strengthen you and move forward in obedience like the men of Tekoa

As the people set their hearts to do the work, the wall was repaired. The rebuilding of the wall required the effort of many. It meant that those who were involved had to be willing to put their own ideas aside. They needed to be humble and learn to work with others. They needed to be willing to get dirty.

God is still looking for willing people today to expand his kingdom. Are you willing to humble yourself and do whatever it takes? Are you willing to let the Lord use you in areas you have never been used before? Are you willing to put aside your pride to work with others? Will you be more concerned about the expansion of the kingdom and obedience to the Lord than your own ideas and desires? If so, God has a role for you. He is looking for men and women who will set everything aside to be obedient. He delights in using this type of person.

For Consideration:

- What encouragement and lessons do you find in the example of the priests who put aside their regular duties to rebuild the wall?

- Have you ever refused to obey because you felt that what God was calling you to do was beneath you? What do we learn here from the nobles of Tekoa?

- How important is it that we learn to function as a team in the work of the kingdom?

- Have you ever felt the Lord calling you to minister in an area where you were not comfortable? What did God teach you through this?

For Prayer:

- Commit yourself to do whatever the Lord calls you to do. Ask the Lord for strength to be obedient.

- Ask the Lord to forgive you for the times you put your own interests and desires before his call in your life.

- Thank the Lord that he wants to use and stretch you in ministry.

- Ask the Lord to help you to work with those he has put beside you in the ministry. Ask him to forgive you for the times you have been a discouragement to others around you.

14

Working and Watching

Read Nehemiah 4:1–23

We saw in the last meditation how God moved his people to rebuild the city wall. This work was not without its difficulties. In chapter 3 we saw how the nobles of Tekoa refused to put their shoulders to the task. The strongest opposition to the rebuilding of the wall, however, came from the enemies of Israel.

Sanballat was an official in the region. In Nehemiah 2:10 we read that he was very much opposed to the rebuilding of the wall of Jerusalem. Sanballat became very angry when he saw the progress being made. He determined in his heart that he would do something to keep this wall from being completed. He began by ridiculing the Jews in an attempt to discourage them.

In the presence of his associates and the army of Samaria, Sanballat asked: "What are those feeble Jews doing? Will they restore their wall? Will they offer sacrifices? Will they finish in a day? Can they bring the stones back to life from those heaps of rubble—burned as they are?" (verse 2). Sanballat questioned the ability of the Jews to rebuild the wall. What we need to understand here is that the Jews who had been spared from the exile and had remained in Judah had been living in this rubble for a long time. For many years this wall had lain in ruins and no one had taken the initiative to do anything about it. The local Jews had come to accept that this was their lot in life. It was only when Nehemiah had challenged them that they began to believe that this wall could go up again.

Sanballat tried to get the Jews to doubt their own abilities. For such a long time, they had lived in defeat. It would not have taken much for them to fall back into that sense of powerlessness. There are many believers like this in our day. They have come to accept defeat in certain areas of their lives. They cannot imagine that their broken marriages could be rebuilt on a proper foundation. They cannot imagine that they could ever have victory over particular habits. As the Lord encourages us to move on and live in victory, the enemy will do all he can to make us doubt that triumph can ever be ours. We have all felt the enemy's mocking.

Sanballat asked: "Can they bring stones back to life?" What Sanballat did not realize was that these simple Jews had the Lord God on their side. The Jews could not bring stones back to life in their own strength, but their God could. The God of Israel is the God of the impossible. In him nothing is too difficult. In him there is hope and victory.

Tobiah the Ammonite was another enemy opposed to the rebuilding of the wall of Jerusalem. He joined Sanballat in mocking the Jews. "What they are building—if even a fox climbed up on it, he would break down their wall of stones!" (verse 3). Tobiah did not expect much from the Jews. He was saying that even if they did build a wall, that wall would not be strong and would quickly fall down.

The fact of the matter was that this was the impression that the Jews had given their enemies. They had been living in humiliation. For seventy years most of them had been living in captivity in Babylon. Those who had remained in Jerusalem had done nothing about the ruins. What was the enemy to think when for seventy years all they had seen was God's people living in rubble or captivity?

What kind of testimony does the church of our day have in the world? What kind of testimony do you have personally? Do people expect great things from you because of your God? Does the enemy fear when he sees you because of the power that is at your disposal as a child of God? Do we understand the power that God offers us for victory in this life?

Faced with the words of the enemy, Nehemiah turned to God and prayed: "Hear us, O our God, for we are despised. Turn their insults back on their own heads. Give them over as plunder in a land of captivity. Do not cover up their guilt or blot out their sins from your sight, for they have thrown insults in the face of the builders" (verses 4–5).

Nehemiah did not seek to defend himself. He did not fight the enemy in his own strength. Instead, he asked God to turn back these insults and deliver the enemy over to captivity. He pleaded with God for justice. The desire of Nehemiah was that the enemy would see the reality of the power of God and would have to swallow all words spoken against the Almighty.

Instead of losing time trying to defend his people, Nehemiah pressed on with the work. Satan would have loved to see Nehemiah enter into a discussion with the enemy. Nehemiah chose not to do so. He committed this problem to the Lord and continued with the task at hand.

These tactics of the enemy to discourage the people did not work. The wall continued to go up. Verse 6 tells us that the "people worked with all their heart" so that the wall reached half its height. Seeing that their efforts did not hinder the rebuilding of the wall, Sanballat and Tobiah became angrier. They determined to strengthen their efforts to obstruct the work. In verse 8 they plot together to find a way of fighting against Jerusalem and stirring up trouble.

It is unclear how word of this came to Nehemiah. In verse 9, however, we learn that Nehemiah decided to post a guard day and night to meet this threat. As the Jews worked, they also watched for the enemy.

There is a lesson for us in this passage. Our enemy Satan has not relented in his efforts against the church. He continually seeks to destroy and discourage the people of God in their labors to build his kingdom. The apostle Peter tells us: "Be self-controlled and alert. Your enemy the devil prowls around like a roaring lion looking for someone to devour" (1 Peter 5:8). We must continue to advance the cause of the Lord in our day. At the same time, we must always be watchful. To put down our guard is to invite the enemy to attack.

The physical labor of rebuilding the wall and the stress of the ever-present enemy was difficult on the Jews. They approached Nehemiah to inform him that the strength of the laborers was giving out, and there was so much rubble that it was becoming impossible to rebuild the wall (verse 10). We should remember that in order for the wall to go up, a lot of rubble needed to be cleared. Simply clearing the old rubble was an overwhelming task.

This is often how it is in our Christian lives. We cannot grow in the Christian faith until we deal with the old rubble of sinful thoughts, attitudes, and habits. We must learn to die to the flesh if we are going to live the new life of the Spirit. Old sins need to be confessed and cleared away so that the new life of Christ can grow. There have been times in my life when I have wondered if this was even possible. It seemed like God was showing me one sin after another that needed to be confessed.

The immensity of the task of reconstructing the wall around Jerusalem combined with the daily threat of the enemy seemed more than the Jews could handle. Success seemed so far removed from these weary builders. They felt the strain of their efforts. In response to this, Nehemiah stationed more people at the vulnerable sections of the wall. All the exposed places were strengthened with guards bearing swords, spears, and bows. In placing guards at the weak points of the wall, Nehemiah accomplished two things. First, he reduced the workload of the builders. They could now focus on construction without also having to watch their backs. Second, he reduced the fear of the builders, enabling them to feel more secure. They could work more efficiently and peacefully.

These weary laborers needed support, and Nehemiah sent them the support they needed. How many weary pastors and Christian workers are there today who feel that same need. I have been in Christian work long enough to realize that there are many weary laborers in the harvest field needing support and encouragement. I have often been among them myself. Maybe you are the answer to the overwhelming need of some lonely workers. Maybe you can be a guard who watches and prays for those vulnerable areas in your pastor's life. Maybe you can encourage a weary laborer.

After sending guards to the weak areas of the wall, Nehemiah stood up and addressed the people. He understood the discouragement they were feeling. He knew the fear that was in their hearts as the enemy threatened them. Addressing those particular needs, Nehemiah challenged his people to remember the faithfulness of God. He reminded them that they had no reason to be afraid. Their God was a great and awesome God. He would fight for them.

Again, the enemy was not pleased that the plot to attack the Jews had been frustrated. God's people were constantly on guard while the work on the wall continued. Verse 16 tells us that half of the Jews worked while the other half kept watch with sword, spear, bow, and armor. Those who carried building material did their work with one hand and held a weapon in the other. All builders wore swords. There was also a man with Nehemiah who was ready to sound a trumpet in the event of an enemy attack. It was agreed that when the trumpet sounded, the nobles, officials, and the rest of the people would gather at the place where it sounded and together they would fight and trust God for victory.

The work continued each day from the first light of morning until the stars came out at night (verse 21). During this time all the Jews slept inside the city. They did not leave Jerusalem for a moment. In this way, the city and the wall were constantly protected. God's people refused to let down their guard. When they went for water, they would take their swords. During that time they did not even take off their clothes.

How easy it would have been for God's people to be discouraged and to let down their defense. The enemy's threat was very real and the reconstruction work was overwhelming. But the Jews gave the enemy absolutely no opportunity to attack. Every weak point was continually fortified with armed guards.

We dare not miss the lesson here. We too need to have such vigilance. We must remain alert because our enemy does not sleep. He is searching for any opportunity to shoot his arrows. God's kingdom must expand, but we must also be very watchful. The people of Nehemiah's day were successful because not only did they work diligently but they protected their labor.

For Consideration:

- Have you ever felt discouraged in the work God has called you to do? What encouragement do you receive from Nehemiah?

- Has your testimony been such that those around you expect great things of you because they know that God is with you?

- What are the weak points that need to be strengthened in your life?

- How aware are we as a church of the spiritual battle that rages around us?

For Prayer:

- Thank the Lord that we can have confidence in him in our times of trouble.

- Do you know Christian workers who have grown weary or overwhelmed by the tasks before them? Ask God to strengthen them and send someone to ease their burdens.

- Ask God to open your eyes to the reality of the spiritual battle that rages around you.

- Commit your weak points to the Lord. Ask him to build you up in those areas.

15

Internal Problems

Read Nehemiah 5:1–19

I n the last chapter, we saw how the people of God were troubled by their enemies as they rebuilt the wall. We saw how the Jews posted guards around the wall to keep watch against an enemy attack. In chapter 5 we see how problems arose inside the city as well.

In those days things were not easy for the people of God in the city of Jerusalem. We understand from verse 3 that there was a famine in the land. Certain Jews came to Nehemiah and explained that they were having a hard time feeding their families. They were in need of grain just to stay alive. Others had to mortgage their fields, vineyards, and homes to get the grain necessary to feed their families.

This lack of food was not the only problem in the land. Some Jews had to borrow money from their brothers and sisters to pay the king's taxes on their fields and vineyards. To pay back what they had borrowed from their brothers and sisters, the poorer Jews had to subject their sons and daughters to slavery (verse 5). Some had even sold their fields and vineyards to pay their debts. The poorer Jews were experiencing severe economic hardship.

When Nehemiah heard these things, he became very angry. He called a meeting of the Jews and spoke to them about this issue. What disturbed him most was how the rich Jews were profiting from the hardship of their poorer brothers and sisters. The wealthy were demanding interest on the loans they had given the poor. Nehemiah reminded the wealthy Jews of how they had just been set free from slavery in Babylon (verse 8), and now they were enslaving their brothers and sisters in Jerusalem. These wealthy Jews were no better than those who had taken them into captivity many years ago. There was an unusual quiet as Nehemiah spoke that day. Those who were guilty knew that Nehemiah spoke the truth. They were guilty as charged.

Nehemiah also reminded the Jews of their responsibility before God to do what was right and to be a witness to the character of God in their actions before unbelievers. Nehemiah made it clear to his fellow Jews that what they were doing did not honor the Lord and did not represent the Lord correctly before the watching world.

The unbelievers are watching us today. The Jews of Nehemiah's day had failed to be the witnesses they should have been because they were mistreating their brothers and sisters. The unbelievers were seeing this and forming a misconception about the God of Israel.

Jesus reminds us in the Gospel of John that the world will know we belong to him by the way we love each other in the church. "By this all men will know that you are my disciples, if you love one another" (John 13:35). This is the challenge to us in our day. The world will form an opinion about the Lord Jesus based on our relationships with each other.

Nehemiah did not condemn the lending of grain. What he did condemn, however, was the outrageous interest. This interest was a heavy burden on the poorer brothers and sisters. Because of this burden, families were losing everything they had.

Nehemiah proposed that all fields, vineyards, olive groves, and houses be given back to their original owners. He also commanded the nobles and rulers to give back the interest they had overcharged their brothers and sisters. Nehemiah understood that it was not enough for the people of God to simply recognize and stop their sin. Something needed to be done to restore what had been taken from the poorer Israelites.

In the Gospel of Luke when Zacchaeus was confronted with his sin of taking more taxes than was necessary, he told Jesus that if he had cheated anyone, he would pay back four times that amount (Luke 19:8). The Law of Moses stated that those who stole were to restore what they had taken plus one-fifth its value. "When a man or woman wrongs another in any way and so is unfaithful to the LORD, that person is guilty and must confess the sin he has committed. He must make full restitution for his wrong, add one fifth to it and give it all to the person he has wronged" (Numbers 5:6–7). It is not enough to confess that we have done wrong. As far as possible, we also need to restore what we have taken from those we have offended.

This is what Nehemiah was proposing to his people. That day the Spirit of God moved in the hearts of his people. They agreed to restore what they had taken and no longer demand interest. To seal this promise, they took an oath before the priests and before God that they would honor their brothers and sisters from that point forward.

To symbolize this agreement, Nehemiah shook out the folds of his robe saying, "In this way may God shake out of his house and possessions every man who does not keep this promise. So may such a man be shaken out and emptied!" (verse 13).

The shaking out of the folds of the one's garment is a graphic symbol. When the folds of the garments were shaken out, anything in those folds was scattered. Nehemiah told the people that if they were unfaithful to the oath they had taken, God would shake out the folds of his garment, and they and all they had would be scattered to the wind.

Nehemiah did not see himself exempt from this oath. As governor in the land of Judah, he refused to eat the food that was customarily allotted to the governor. Unlike other governors, he made the burden easy for the people of Judah. Nehemiah devoted himself to working on the wall. He did not demand land for himself. Each day he fed one hundred and fifty Jews. Officials ate at his table as well as many foreigners. Every day an ox, six sheep, and poultry were prepared for him and his servants to eat. Nehemiah was very open and accountable to God and to Judah for how he used his resources. Nehemiah dedicated himself to being hospitable and gracious in his dealings with the people of Judah.

The concern of Nehemiah was how he could use his position to minister and bless the people of God. He willingly sacrificed his rights as governor so that others could have more resources. This sacrificial attitude was a key component in the success of his ministry. May God give us more leaders like Nehemiah, willing to sacrifice their rights and comforts for the sake of the Lord's work.

Satan attempted to divide brothers and sisters in the city of Jerusalem. He knew that if he could break their spirits and cause them to become bitter and angry at each other, then the work of the kingdom would suffer. Satan uses this same technique today. Nehemiah understood the seriousness of this problem and did what was necessary to restore relationships. In this way, the Lord's work could advance.

For Consideration:

- Take a moment to consider the relationships you have in the body of Christ today. Are there any broken relationships you need to mend?

- What is the connection between our relationships with brothers and sisters in Christ and our witness in the world?

- What do we learn about the importance of not only confessing our sin but also making things right?

- What do we learn from the example of Nehemiah's leadership?

For Prayer:

- Ask the Lord to show you if there is a brother or sister you have offended. Ask him to give you strength and wisdom to make things right with this person.

- Ask the Lord to help you to be willing to sacrifice your rights for the sake of the body of Christ, as did Nehemiah.

- Thank the Lord for the way he is able to use us to overcome the attacks of the enemy against the church.

- Take a moment to ask the Lord to protect the relationships in your church. Ask him to teach you to love and bless those he puts in your path.

16

Personal Attacks

Read Nehemiah 6:1–19

The work of rebuilding the wall of Jerusalem had not been without its difficulties. Each day the Samaritan leaders had threatened the people of God with ridicule and threats of physical violence. The Jews had responded by continuing to rebuild the wall and by working with swords hung at their sides in preparation for an enemy attack. The enemies of God had done their best to discourage the Jews in their efforts to complete the Lord's work, but the Jews had continued to move forward. When the Samaritan leaders saw that these efforts were to no avail, they changed tactics. In this chapter the Samaritan enemy decides to personally attack Nehemiah, the leader of the Jews.

We need to realize that leaders will often be subject to the attack of the enemy. Satan knows that when a leader falls, the people will not be far behind. The personal attacks on Nehemiah began when Sanballat, Tobiah, and Geshem heard that the wall had been completed except for the doors in the gates. Sanballat and Geshem sent a message to Nehemiah asking him to meet with them in one of the villages on the Plain of Ono in the territory of Benjamin. This meant that Nehemiah would have had to leave the city of Jerusalem and the work of reconstruction there. Verse 2 tells us that hidden behind this invitation was a scheme to harm Nehemiah.

Nehemiah was suspicious of the invitation. More than that, however, he knew that in his absence the work would stop. God had called him to complete this work and he refused to leave it until the work was finished. The enemies sent an invitation four times to Nehemiah, but each time he refused. Satan knows that while we may resist his temptations once, the more he keeps tempting us, the more likely we are to finally give in. Therefore, he perseveres in his attacks. Nehemiah, however, resisted the persistent temptation and each time returned the same answer.

The fifth time the messenger came, he handed Nehemiah an unsealed letter. The fact that this letter was unsealed is significant. When a letter was sealed, the contents were hidden from everyone but the writer and the reader. This unsealed letter was like a postcard we might send in the mail. The contents were for anyone to read. Sanballat was warning Nehemiah that the contents of this letter had been made public.

In the unsealed letter, Sanballat told Nehemiah that he had heard that the Jews under his leadership were plotting a revolt. This was totally unfounded. Sanballat also accused Nehemiah of wanting to become the king of the Jews and of already appointing prophets to proclaim him king in Judah. Sanballat reminded Nehemiah that this report would very quickly get back to the king of Persia who would waste no time in sending his army to destroy the Jews. Having said this, Sanballat once again invited Nehemiah to meet with him. The intention of Sanballat was to scare Nehemiah into coming to see him so that the Samaritan leaders could do him serious harm.

This letter, however, did not threaten Nehemiah. He told Sanballat that all these accusations were only the imaginations of his mind. Nehemiah understood that the only reason for this letter was to cause the Jews to fear and stop the work (verse 9).

Though Sanballat's letter had not intimidated Nehemiah, he took it very seriously. In verse 9 Nehemiah went to God to ask him for strength to continue the work. As a human being, Nehemiah felt these threats deeply; but as a servant of God, he was not going to give into the enemy's attacks. He cried out to God for the strength necessary to complete the task and resist the enemy.

It is noteworthy that Nehemiah came to God for that strength. The apostle James tells us in James 4:2 that we do not have because we do not ask. God's strength was available to Nehemiah, but he needed to ask him for it. How many times have we failed to receive from God because we did not ask? What do you need to accomplish the task that God wants you to accomplish? God is willing to give you all you need if you will come to him and ask.

One day Nehemiah went to the house of a prophet by the name of Shemaiah. Shemaiah had secluded himself in his home. It is unclear what the purpose of this isolation was. Shemaiah told Nehemiah that there were men seeking to kill him. This word was obviously true. Shemaiah then proceeded to tell Nehemiah to hide himself in the temple for protection.

Nehemiah refused to listen to the counsel of Shemaiah. There are several possible reasons for this. First, if Nehemiah locked himself in the temple, he would be admitting that his God was not able to protect him. This would have sent a message of fear and defeat to the people under him. Second, if Nehemiah hid in the temple, he would have to withdraw from the work God had called him to do. The people would be left without a leader. Nehemiah did not feel that it would be proper to run away from the task to which God had called him. He needed to set an example for his people, and he was willing to die to do that. He feared God more than then he feared losing his life.

Notice that the enemy put a religious twist on this temptation by using a prophet. Satan will not hesitate to hide behind religious language. We need to realize that he will use any method he can to accomplish his purposes. In Acts 5 Ananias and Sapphira came to the apostles with a gift. To all outward appearances, this was a wonderful thing. What was unseen to the human eye, however, was that Satan had put it on their hearts to lie to the Holy Spirit and to the church. We need to avoid being deceived by those who use religious language to accomplish the enemy's purposes. It was not long before Nehemiah realized that the enemy had hired Shemaiah to deceive and discredit him before the people (verses 12–13).

There were many other personal attacks on Nehemiah in those days. In verse 14 Nehemiah mentions other prophets who tried to intimidate him. Mention is made of the prophetess Noadiah in particular. The enemy was using the religious people of the day for evil purposes. Nehemiah not only had to be aware of attacks from external enemies but also from internal enemies as well. Maybe you have experienced attacks from inside your church. Any pastor knows the struggle of maintaining unity and harmony in the body of Christ. Satan does his best to attack from every angle.

Despite all the efforts of the enemy, God's people completed the wall in fifty-two days. When their enemies saw that the wall was completed, they became afraid and lost confidence. Despite tremendous obstacles God's people had persevered and accomplished the impossible. The enemy understood that this work had been completed with the help of the Lord God. The completion of this wall was a clear sign to the enemy that the Lord God was with his people. This did not mean that the Jews would not face more difficulties, but it did mean that God would give the Jews all they needed to finish the work he had called them to do.

The tasks to which God has called us will require much effort and struggle at times. We may have to face our share of difficulties and pain. God does not promise that we will never have struggles, but he does promise to get us through each of those struggles if we persevere and continue in obedience. Isaiah 43:2 is a clear example of this: "When you pass through the waters, I will be with you; and when you pass through the rivers they will not sweep over you. When you walk through the fire, you will not be burned; the flames will not set you ablaze."

Notice in verses 17-19 that Tobiah tried to undermine Nehemiah's authority by continually sending letters to the Jewish nobles in order to develop good relationships with them. The nobles fell into this trap and listened to what Tobiah was saying. Many of these leaders came to Nehemiah, reporting to him all the good deeds of Tobiah. At the same time, Tobiah was sending letters to Nehemiah, trying to intimidate him. Tobiah was gaining the favor of the nobles and at the same time trying to destroy Nehemiah's reputation and leadership. Tobiah was an instrument in the hand of Satan to undermine the work of God's chosen servant. One day Tobiah would have to answer to God for this. The nobles did not understand what was happening. Although Tobiah did many wonderful things and gained the respect of the nobles of the land, in reality, he was a tool of Satan. How easy it is for us to be deceived. How we need the discernment of God if we are to see his kingdom expand. Nehemiah had that discernment and did not fail in the ministry to which God had called him.

For Consideration:

- What do we learn about the tactics of the enemy to destroy the work of God?

- How does the enemy seek to distract you from your calling?

- What do we learn about the reality of difficulties and trials in the work of God?

- Have you ever seen evidence of Satan using people in the church to hinder the work of God? Explain.

- What do we learn in this chapter about the need for discernment and strength from the Lord?

For Prayer:

- Ask the Lord to give you greater discernment to recognize the presence of the enemy and his attacks.

- Ask God to bring a greater sense of unity and harmony to the body of Christ.

- Ask God for perseverance and strength to face the difficulties before you right now.

- Take a moment to pray for your spiritual leaders. Ask God to protect and keep them. Ask him to give them strength and discernment to face the opposition of the enemy, as they seek to advance his kingdom.

17

Settled in Jerusalem

Read Nehemiah 7:1–73

The city wall of Jerusalem had been rebuilt. Nehemiah had completed the task the Lord his God had given him to do. The road to the completion of the wall had been a long one. It had begun with a burden on Nehemiah's heart while he was still in exile. God had wonderfully opened the door for him to return to Jerusalem. With the blessing of the king of Persia, Nehemiah had returned to his homeland with a number of Israelites. He had persevered through many difficulties and personal attacks to complete the rebuilding of the wall in less than two months. This had not been the effort of Nehemiah alone. God's people, as a whole, had submitted to Nehemiah's leadership and persevered in this massive undertaking. God had blessed their efforts and the work had been completed.

Now that the work on the wall was completed, Nehemiah set his heart to creating some order in the city. His first task was to appoint leadership. He appointed gatekeepers, singers, and Levites to minister and protect the city. Nehemiah also appointed his brother Hanani to be in charge of the city of Jerusalem. He named Hananiah as commander of the citadel. Verse 2 makes it very clear that the reason he appointed these men was because they were men of integrity who feared God more than most men did. Nehemiah knew he could trust them to deal honestly with the people and lead them in the ways of the Lord.

Nehemiah's priorities were right. His concern was that the people of Israel live in obedience to the Lord God in this city of Jerusalem. Nehemiah knew that this would be the basis of their success as a people. God would honor those who honored him and lived in obedience to his commands (Deuteronomy 4:40; 28:1-2).

In verse 3 Nehemiah commanded that the gates of the city be closed at night and remain closed until the sun was hot. We need to remember that Israel's enemies were not content to see the Israelites return to their homeland. These enemies would take advantage of any opportunity to attack the city. The gates were closed each night to protect the people inside the wall. Those gates would remain closed until the sun had come up and everyone was out of bed and alert. That way, should the enemy attack, God's people would be ready.

Not only were the gates to be closed and protected but Nehemiah commanded that residents of Jerusalem be appointed to guard a section of wall near their own homes. In this way, the city would always be on guard and ready to face the enemy. Jerusalem was to be in a constant state of readiness.

We need to understand that this same principle applies to our own walk with the Lord. While those who have accepted the Lord Jesus are surrounded by the wall of salvation, this does not mean that we can let down our guard. Our enemy Satan is constantly seeking an opportunity to ensnare us or devour us. The apostle Peter warns Christians in 1 Peter 5:8:

"Be self-controlled and alert. Your enemy the devil prowls around like a roaring lion looking for someone to devour." For this reason, we need to be constantly on guard. Satan will do anything he can to cause us to wander off the path of righteousness, although we cannot lose our salvation.

At this time, though the wall of the city had been rebuilt, many homes were still in disrepair. The city was large, but there were only a few people living in it. There was much work to be done. In some ways, this is not unlike our walk with God. Salvation is only the beginning for us. I am discovering that though my salvation is sure, I still have much work to do in my life. There are areas of my life that need to be repaired and healed. In order to grow in faith, I need to place my confidence and trust in the Lord. Faith will increase as I learn to be even more obedient. The wall of salvation has been completed, and I am now surrounded by God's forgiveness and grace. But I have to work inside this wall, repairing and restoring what has been broken down by the enemy. This is a lifelong process.

The Lord put it on the heart of Nehemiah to register all those who had returned from the exile. It is important to notice that Nehemiah took his direction from the Lord God. Nehemiah's strong relationship with the Lord allowed him to be directed in specific ways. I have often wrestled with this in my personal life. I would love to be at a place in my walk with the Lord that I could know clearly his leading and direction in some specific matters. I suppose that all of us struggle to know the specific will of God at any given moment. Nehemiah heard the Lord God and responded in obedience.

The names of those who had returned from captivity were recorded. The nobles and the people gathered in the city of Jerusalem for this registration. It is interesting to compare this with what John the apostle wrote in the book of Revelation. In Revelation 20:12–21:3 John speaks about a book of life where the names of those who belong to the New Jerusalem are written. All those whose names are written in that book of life are given access to the heavenly Jerusalem. While this passage in Nehemiah does not speak of the New Jerusalem, the comparison is still very real.

The wonderful truth for us today is that if we have come to the Lord Jesus for forgiveness and have experienced his salvation, our names are registered in that book of life. Like the people in Jerusalem in the days of Nehemiah, we have been freed from the land of bondage and our names are written in the registry of those who belong to the New Jerusalem. Nothing can take that citizenship from us.

Notice in verse 61 that there were certain individuals who could not show that their families were descendants of Israel. In verse 64 there were priests who could not prove their priesthood by family records. These priests were forbidden to eat the sacred food or to minister until it could be proved by Urim and Thummim that they were true priests called of God. The Urim and Thummim were small objects carried by a priest for the purpose of determining the will of the Lord in specific situations. It is possible that they were special stones through which God would communicate his will and purpose. We see reference to these articles in Exodus 28:30, Leviticus 8:8, and Numbers 27:21 but it is uncertain how they were used.

The number of people who were registered at that time was 42,360. Beyond this number were 7,337 servants and 245 singers. These individuals had 736 horses, 245 mules, 435 camels, and 6,720 donkeys. A record was also made of the contributions of the governor and the heads of various families in verses 70-72. After this registration the people retuned to their various towns and settled down.

Nehemiah's concern was to provide Israel with a godly and mature leadership. He chose men whom he could trust to lead his people into the path of righteousness. He realized that completing the wall was not sufficient. If Jerusalem was to become the city it had once been, there was much work to do in the city itself. Through registering the people, it was discovered that there were individuals who could not prove their right to be priests. These individuals were removed from their positions. Nehemiah's concern was for the glory of God, and he did everything in his power to facilitate obedience to the Word of the Lord and remove all that would hinder that obedience.

For Consideration:

- What do we learn about Nehemiah's concern for righteousness and integrity in the land?

- What is the connection between obedience to God and blessing in the land?

- What do we learn about the importance of being constantly on guard in our walk with God?

- Why was it important that those who could not prove their priesthood be removed from their positions?

- What does this chapter teach us about the work that needs to be done in our lives after we come to know the Lord? How can we compare the city of Jerusalem to our own spiritual lives?

For Prayer:

- Ask the Lord to restore honesty and godliness in your land. Ask him to give you spiritual and civil leaders who are honest and live righteous lives.

- Ask God to help you to be on guard in your walk with him.

- Ask the Lord to show you anything in your life that needs to be repaired or restored to him. Ask him for strength to do whatever is necessary to have victory in those areas of your life.

- Take a moment to thank the Lord that he has surrounded you by the wall of salvation. Thank him that you can have complete assurance of his salvation in your life.

18

A Gathering in the Square

Read Nehemiah 8:1–12

I n the last chapter, Nehemiah chose leaders with integrity to minister to the people in Jerusalem. He had a deep concern, as a servant of God, to see his people walk in the ways of the Lord.

In the first part of chapter 8, the people assemble in the square before the Water Gate. From verse 2 we understand that this day is the first day of the seventh month. We discover in Leviticus 23:24 that this was a special Jewish celebration. "On the first day of the seventh month you are to have a day of rest, a sacred assembly commemorated with trumpet blasts." This day was known as the Feasts of Trumpets. It is believed to have been a celebration of the civil new year.

As the people stood in the square, Ezra the priest and scribe brought out the Book of the Law of Moses. Ezra stood on a high wooden platform with a number of religious leaders beside him. As he opened up the Book of the Law, the people rose to their feet in respect. Ezra read from the Book of the Law from daybreak until noon. The people listened attentively.

God moved in power among his people and Ezra led them in praise. The people responded by raising their hands and crying: "Amen! Amen!" Then they bowed down with their faces to the ground and worshiped. God's people were obviously being touched by the Lord as they listened to his Word that day.

As the Word was read, the Levites circulated among the people, explaining the meaning of the Word so that it could be clearly applied. The people were so touched by what they had heard that many of them broke down and wept before the Lord. Nehemiah challenged them to cease their grieving and go have something to eat and drink. He reminded them that the joy of the Lord was their strength (verse 10).

In response, the Levites moved among the people we were grieving and helped them to calm down. The people listened to Nehemiah and Ezra and then sat down to eat and drink. Together they celebrated with great joy because the Lord had made his Word clear to them.

There are a couple of things we need to notice. First, we need to see the exhortation of Nehemiah to those who were grieving to cease from their grief and rejoice in the Lord. Nehemiah told them that their strength was in the joy of the Lord. We need to examine this for a moment.

Those present that day were touched and very likely convicted by the words they heard from the Book of the Law. God was revealing to them that they had fallen short of his standard. As they listened to the requirements of God, the Spirit of God convicted them. They grieved to realize that they had fallen short of God's standard. It is important that we all come to this point in our lives.

Nehemiah advised his people, however, that they move from grief to joy. Nehemiah understood that as long as God's people remained in this state of grief and brokenness, they would never advance in their walk with God. Satan knows that if he can keep believers focused only on their sin, they will never have the courage to stand up and advance the kingdom. I have met believers (and for many years I was one of them) who have not understood the nature of forgiveness. They live for years with guilt when God has covered their sin and cast it far from them.

Satan wants us to be defeated by our sin. He wants us to believe that God could never accept us or use us. Many believers are deceived by Satan's lies and do not move forward in forgiveness and renewal to accomplish great things for the kingdom.

Nehemiah reminded his people that there was victory over sin and that the joy of the Lord was their strength. This joy is our strength too. This joy comes from the knowledge of forgiveness and acceptance in the eyes of God. There is no need for us to be discouraged because God offers us victory. As unworthy as we are, we have been chosen by God. He delights in equipping and enabling us. In him we can conquer every temptation the enemy throws at us. Satan fears believers who understand their position in Christ. He fears those who joyfully understand that they are children of a gracious God.

While the path of joy crosses the valley of grief, it rises beyond that valley to the mountains of acceptance, forgiveness, and enabling. Beyond the cross is the resurrection. Beyond the wilderness is the Promised Land. While we must all come to an awareness of our sin, God does not want us to remain in that valley of defeat. He calls us on to the joyful experience of victory and grace.

There is one more point that we should mention in this passage. Notice that the reason for joy in the hearts of God's people is because they had come to an understanding of the truth of the Word of God. Here were people who for many years had never grasped the truth of God's Law. That day, however, the Lord made his Word clear to them. They left that sacred assembly with a new appreciation for the wonderful privilege of having the sacred Scriptures. God's Word had broken them but also given them clear direction and guidance. The Law revealed to them the meaning of life and the purposes of God for them. Before this, God's Word had meant very little to them. In some cases it had no doubt proved a bother to them, especially when it revealed their sin. On that day, however, they rediscovered the awesomeness of the Lord's holy Word.

Have we understood the treasure we have in the Word of God? Maybe we need to rediscover the joy of this Word, as did the people of Nehemiah's day.

For Consideration:

- What evidence was there of the presence of the Spirit of God in the gathering of the people in the square by the Water Gate?

- What was the result of the reading of the Book of the Law?

- What difference does the joy of the Lord make in our lives?

- What reason do we have to be joyful as believers today?

- What does this passage tell us about the power of the Word of God?

For Prayer:

- Thank the Lord that he left us with his Word in written form.

- Ask the Lord to give you a deeper appreciation for his Word.

- Thank the Lord that you have forgiveness and victory in him.

- Ask the Lord to fill you with joy.

19

A Forgotten Feast

Read Nehemiah 8:13–18

God had been doing a wonderful work in the lives of his people. Many had been broken by the public reading of the Word of God. There had been great rejoicing on that day. The Word of God had come alive to them.

The next day the people gathered again to hear the words of the Law of God. On that occasion, they found written in the Law that the Israelites were to live in booths during the feast of the seventh month. It appears from this that the practice of living in booths had been forgotten. We read about the command of the Lord for the Israelites to live in booths in the book of Leviticus: "Live in booths for seven days: All native-born Israelites are to live in booths so your descendants will know that I had the Israelites live in booths when I brought them out of Egypt. I am the LORD your God" (Leviticus 23:42–43).

This command of the Lord to live in booths had been given through Moses. Israel was to practice the celebration yearly as a remembrance of how their ancestors lived when they passed through the wilderness on their way to the Promised Land. We need to see how patient God had been with his people during the many years they had not obeyed this commandment. How thankful we ought to be to God who patiently bears with all of us in our disobedience and failures.

God's people had been living in ignorance of his Word. They had lost the practice of celebrating the Feast of Booths. They had not been taught the truth of his Word and were living in ignorance of its principles.

When the people heard the Law of God from Ezra that day, they determined that they would obey the command of God. They went out and brought back branches to build the booths. They placed the booths anywhere they could find a place. Some set up their booths on the flat roofs of their houses. Others set them up in their courtyards. Those who did not have a place to set up their booths did so in the temple courtyard or in the squares by the Water Gate and the Gate of Ephraim.

Notice in verse 17 that there was great joy among the people of God that day. There was joy in obedience to the Word of the Lord. Admittedly, there was a sacrifice to be made in leaving the comfort of their own beds to live in booths on the roofs of their houses and other places. However, the Lord's people made that sacrifice with joy in their hearts. The privilege of obedience far outweighed the sacrifice of comfort. Willing sacrifice will always bring joy to our hearts. For the seventy years of exile, God's people had been missing the privilege of celebrating this Feast of Booths. When it was rediscovered, it brought great joy and satisfaction to their hearts. For seven days the children of Israel lived in these booths and heard Ezra read from the

Book of the Law of God. On the eighth day, they gathered for a great assembly.

Nehemiah had reminded the people in verse 10 that the joy of the Lord was their strength. God's intention has always been that his people experience this joy in celebration and praise of him. This is what the people of Nehemiah's day were experiencing. May God grant that we would rediscover this joy of celebrating his goodness.

For Consideration:

• What do we learn here about the patience of God?

• How important is it that we remember the things God has done for us in the past? How does this help us to live in the present?

• What does this passage teach us about the joy of sacrifice?

• What do we learn here about the intention of God that we live in joyful obedience?

• What is the connection between obedience and joy?

For Prayer:

• Thank the Lord for his patience with you.

• Ask the Lord to help you rediscover joy in your walk and service for him.

• Take a moment to remember the good things the Lord has done for you. Thank him for these things.

20

Rebellious People, Faithful God

Read Nehemiah 9:1–38

The children of Israel had rediscovered the Feast of Booths (or the Feast of Tabernacles). Beginning on the fifteenth day of the seventh month and lasting for seven days, the Israelites were to live in booths made from gathered branches. They were to do this in memory of how their ancestors had lived as they had wandered through the desert. On the twenty-fourth day of the seventh month, the people were to conclude the Feast of Booths by holding a sacred assembly with prayers, a reading of the Law, and a confession of sin (see Leviticus 23:33–43).

It was on the day of this concluding sacred assembly that the Israelites gathered (verse 1). They mourned over their sins by fasting, wearing sackcloth, and throwing dust on their heads. In preparation for this day, the Israelites had separated themselves from all foreigners. Those who had married foreign wives separated from those wives according to the command of God. This was an assembly for the people of God. No unbeliever was to attend. Israelites who had married foreign wives or had made an alliance with foreigners stood up and confessed their disobedience.

As the people stood before the Lord that day, the Book of the Law was read. For a quarter of the day, they listened to the reading of the Law of God. They spent another quarter of the day confessing their sins and praising God. What a wonderful day that was.

The Levites stood on the stairs and called out with loud voices to the Lord God, so all could hear. They praised God for being an everlasting God having no beginning or end. They recognized that the name of the Lord their God is exalted above all blessing and praise. The Levites could find no words of praise or blessing that could match the worth of their Lord. The Levites worshiped the Lord because he is the creator of the heavens with all their stars and the earth with all that is on it. They blessed him as the creator of the seas and everything in them. They confessed him to be the creator of all the angels of heaven who praise his name.

Having recognized him as the creator of all things, the Levites worshiped God for his gracious role in the lives of his people. The Levites recounted a brief history of Israel for the gathered people (verses 7-31). The Levites recalled that the Lord chose Abram to be his instrument. God brought him out of Ur and gave him the name of Abraham meaning "father of a multitude." God made a covenant with Abraham, promising to make from him a great nation. God promised to give Abraham's descendants the land of the Canaanites, Hittites, Amorites, Perizzites, Jebusites and Girgashites. God kept that promise, and Abraham and his descendants settled in the land of Canaan.

When God's people were in Egypt under the cruel domination of Pharaoh, God heard their cry and set them free. He opened a door through the Red Sea and, through many signs and wonders, defeated Egypt and made a glorious name for himself. The Lord sent his people through the divided sea on dry land, delivering them from Egypt. The Egyptians tried to follow Israel but were drowned as the waters of the sea collapsed on them.

God led his people through the desert by means of a pillar of cloud by day and a pillar of fire by night. At Mount Sinai he gave them his laws and regulations. By following these laws, God's people would honor their God and be a light to the nations around them.

Not only did God guide his people through the wilderness he also provided for their basic needs of food and water. He gave them manna from heaven and water from a rock. God led his people through the wilderness to the land he had promised to Abraham. The Lord was faithful to all his promises. He cared for his people and delivered them from all their enemies.

Despite these wonderful blessings, God's people became proud and did not listen to God or obey his commands. The Israelites quickly forgot the wonderful miracles God had performed on their behalf. They were not content with what God had given them and appointed a leader to take them back to the land of slavery.

Despite this insult, God was very gracious to them. Because of his love for his people, he did not desert them in their rebellion. In the desert they made a golden calf and claimed that this idol was the god who brought them out of Egypt. Again, despite their blasphemy, God showed great patience with them and did not destroy them.

As the Levites continued to pray aloud that day, they praised the Lord for his wonderful compassion and love for his people. The Levites recalled that God's grace and mercy had extended over a period of forty years when the Israelites did not lack anything. Their clothes did not wear out and their feet did not become swollen.

Despite their continued rebellion against him, God gave his people whole kingdoms and nations. The Israelites became a fruitful people and were blessed with many children. Their descendants became as numerous as the stars of the sky. Their children entered the land that God had promised to his people. God gave them victory over all their enemies. They took possession of homes filled with many wonderful things. Their wells were already dug for them. In that Promised Land, vineyards, olive groves, and fruit trees were in abundance. The Israelites had all they needed to eat. They were well nourished and enjoyed the goodness of God in the land he had promised them.

Once again, however, they were disobedient to his Law. God sent his prophets to warn them, but they killed these prophets. In his anger God turned them over to their enemies who oppressed them. In their oppression they cried out to God and he heard their request. He sent deliverers to set them free.

As soon as they had rest from their enemies, however, God's people returned to their evil ways. God's blessing was again removed from them. They again cried out to God, and God heard their request and delivered them. This cycle continued for many years.

God told them that they would be blessed only by obedience to his Word, but they chose to turn their backs on him and his ways. They refused to listen to him, even though it meant they would perish in their sin. Though God could have put an end to the nation of Israel, he chose to be merciful and preserve a remnant through whom he would continue to work.

As the Levites stood before the people that day and prayed, there was an awareness that they had been granted the favor of God to return to their land only because of his great grace and mercy. As a people, they had rebelled repeatedly against the Lord God. They did not deserve the favor of the Lord. The Israelites who returned from exile realized that they were no better than their ancestors who had turned their backs on God and his ways. The Levites confessed that day that God had been absolutely just and righteous in punishing them.

Though God had granted his people the privilege of returning to their own land, they were still subjects of the king of Persia. The Israelites realized that while this land should have been completely theirs, its harvests were still going to the king of Persia in tribute and taxes. The Israelites were still not where they wanted to be, as the people of God. A foreign king ruled over them and their cattle. The Jews were not content simply to return to their homeland. They believed that God still had more for them than what they were presently experiencing. They wanted to see an even greater work of God. They wanted complete victory and freedom from the power of the enemy in their land.

There is a powerful lesson here for us. All too many of us have been content with a Christianity that is like the city of Jerusalem in that day. The city was still in ruins. Its inhabitants were still under the domination of a foreign king. Many Christians live like this today. They have become content to live in a sense of defeat. Their walk with God is not what it should be. The enemy still has strongholds in their lives, but they have determined that this is normal.

The Jews of Nehemiah's day determined that they would not stand idly by and live in defeat. They determined that day to do something about their situation (verse 38). Together they made a binding agreement before God to live in obedience to his Word so that once again they could know the fullness of his victory in their lives. May God give us Christians like this today.

For Consideration:

- What do we learn here about the compassion and grace of God?

- What was the result of disobedience to the Lord in the lives of his people? What is the result in our lives today?

- Should God punish his people for sin?

- What challenge did the Levites bring to the people that day? Were God's people content to live in defeat?

- Have you been living in defeat as a believer? Is there victory in your life?

For Prayer:

- Thank the Lord for his great faithfulness even when you have rebelled against him.

- Take a moment to confess your sin before the Lord and accept his forgiveness.

- Ask the Lord to reveal any area of spiritual defeat in your life. Ask him for victory.

- Ask God to keep you from being content to live in defeat. Ask him to help you live in constant victory over the enemy and his attacks.

21

A Binding Agreement

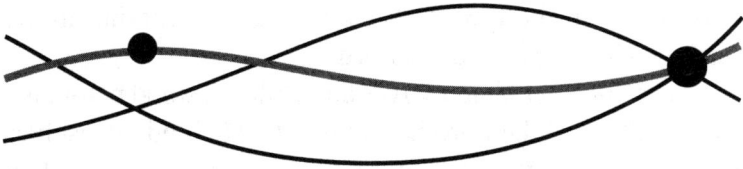

Read Nehemiah 10:1–39

I n chapter 9 the people of God celebrated the final day of the Feast of Booths. On that day they read from the Book of the Law, praised the Lord, and confessed their sin. The Levites called the people's attention to the fact that their ancestors had turned their backs on God and his purposes, and they reminded the people that their own personal response to the Lord had not been any better. This acknowledgment moved the people's hearts to action. Together they agreed to a binding agreement to honor and serve the Lord faithfully. In chapter 10 we see the nature of this agreement.

Verses 1-29 give us a list of the people who bound themselves to this agreement before God. At the top of the list are Nehemiah, and the priests (verses 1–8). This is followed by the names of the Levites and their associates (verses 9–13). Following the Levites is a list of leaders (verses 14–27) and finally, in verse 28 is a listing of the rest of the people who bound themselves to the agreement. It is important to note that those who joined this agreement separated themselves from their foreign neighbors. Those who had married foreign wives or had other unhealthy associations with unbelievers needed to break those ties before they could bind themselves to this agreement. Among those who had broken this command of God to keep themselves separate from the nations were priests, Levites, gatekeepers, singers, and temple servants as well as ordinary people. There were spiritual leaders who were not living in harmony with the Law of the Lord but still serving in the temple. This displeased the Lord.

These men with their wives and children stood before the Lord and joined their brothers and sisters to bind themselves to a spiritual covenant before God. Notice in verse 29 that they bound themselves with a curse and an oath. They made their promise to God, realizing that if they turned from that promise, the curse of God would fall on them. They pledged their lives to this promise.

That day these individuals bound themselves to follow the Law of God as given through Moses. They promised to obey all the laws of God and follow every command, regulation, and decree. God moved the hearts of his people to live in absolute obedience. They understood how rebellious their fathers and mothers had been. They saw clearly from the reading of the Book of the Law how the disobedience of their fathers and mothers had brought the wrath of God on their nation. That day God's people chose to do things differently.

Of particular note is the reference to several key past failures. In verse 30 reference is made to the practice of marrying foreign wives. In those days many men had to separate from their foreign wives. They realized that they were not living in obedience to the Lord in this matter. They confessed their sin and made a solemn vow never to marry their daughters or sons to the foreigners around them. God's desire was to see a people who were pure and free from the pagan practices these foreign spouses would bring to their families.

Verse 31 refers to the practice of the Sabbath. Those present with Nehemiah that day promised before God that when their neighbors brought merchandise or grain to sell in the city on the Sabbath, they would not buy it. Instead, they would honor the Sabbath and keep it as a day for worship and rest.

Also part of the Sabbath law was the practice of allowing the land to rest every seventh year (Exodus 23:10–11). In that year the Israelites were also required to cancel all debts (Deuteronomy 15:1–2). These people committed themselves to serving the Lord no matter the cost.

Those who bound themselves to this agreement consented to give money to the work of the temple of God. They promised to bring a third of a shekel each year for the service of the house of God. It is interesting to note that God commanded his people in Exodus 30:11–16 to bring one-half a shekel for the service of the temple. The people of Nehemiah's day only committed themselves to giving one-third. This means that they were not giving what Moses recommended. It is quite likely that this was due to the poverty of the time and their living conditions.

Notice in verse 33 that this money would go to the purchase of bread to be set out on the table, the various animal sacrifices that took place during the year, and the numerous other expenses of the house of the Lord. The priests cast lots to determine when each family was to bring a contribution of wood to burn on the altar for the sacrifices. This responsibility was shared among the people.

In verse 35 the people committed themselves to bring the firstfruits of their crops and fruit trees as an offering to the Lord God in recognition of his provision. They also agreed to bring the firstborn of their sons and their cattle to the house of the Lord. This practice was established when the Israelites left Egypt. On that day the Lord killed the firstborn of every family that did not have the blood of a lamb sprinkled on the doorpost (Exodus 12:12-13). From that day forward, as a commemoration of the Passover, God required his people to give to him the firstborn from the womb. Firstborn children were to be redeemed at a cost (Exodus 13:13–15).

In verse 37 the people bound themselves to bringing the first of their meal, grain, fruit trees, wine, and oil to the temple as an offering to the Lord. What is important for us to note here is that the Lord requires the first portion of what we have. Very often, we give him what is left over. Before we use anything for ourselves, God wants us to set his part aside. He desires to have the priority in the use of our money and resources.

The people of Nehemiah's day bound themselves to give one-third of a shekel per year for the work of the temple. They also dedicated the firstfruits and firstborn of their crops, animals, and children to the Lord. They renewed their commitment to also give a tithe of their crops to the work of the Lord. The Levites would gather tithes at the allotted time and place them in the storerooms of the temple.

Other contributions were also to be made during the course of the year. God's people committed themselves also to bring grain, new wine, and oil to the storerooms of the temple as the Lord led them. These contributions were above the other commitments they made to the Lord that day. They promised that they would not neglect God's house.

We can see that the Spirit of God was moving among his people that day. Men and women were touched by God. The result of this move of God's Spirit was that his people offered themselves afresh to him. They committed themselves to obey God's laws and willingly gave back to the Lord from all he had given them. May God give us this same heart today.

For Consideration:

- What do we learn in this chapter about the desire of the Lord God that we offer our possessions and ourselves to him?

- Consider the sacrifices the people of Nehemiah's day were willing to make. What sacrifice are you willing to make today for the sake of the kingdom of God?

- Is there any way in which you have fallen from your first commitment to the Lord God? Could it be that you need to renew your commitment to the Lord, as did the people in Nehemiah's day?

For Prayer:

- Ask the Lord to open your heart to see any area where you have fallen short in your commitment to him.

- Thank the Lord for the blessings he has given you.

- Ask the Lord to help you to be more willing to sacrifice what he has given you for the sake of his kingdom.

- Ask the Lord to forgive you for the areas of your life where you have not been as faithful to him as you should have been.

- Ask him to show you his will for the use of the resources he has given you today.

22

The People Settle in the Land

Read Nehemiah 11:1–36

I f the city of Jerusalem was to become the great city that it had once been, it was important that the population of the city increase. There was much work to be done to repair the city. This required people with various skills and trades. The question of who was to settle in Jerusalem had to be examined.

While it was an honor to live in the city of Jerusalem, we need to remember that land and property would be more limited in the confines of the city. We also need to remember that the city of Jerusalem had been the focus of the enemy's attacks. Those living in the city would have to commit themselves to defend it. During the construction of the wall, builders had worked with their swords at their sides. Those who lived in the city needed to be people of courage who were willing to face the enemy as well as work hard to rebuild the city to restore it to its former glory. Not everyone would have been willing to do this. Many, no doubt, would have preferred to live in the peaceful and relatively secure towns outside of the city.

Jerusalem would be the center of government. This meant that the leaders were to settle in the city. Because the temple was located in the city, some of the priests and religious leaders would also need to live in the city.

The people who willingly agreed to remain in the city of Jerusalem were commended as honorable Israelites. This was a high honor. It was bestowed on them because they were willing to put aside their own interests for the benefit of the nation as a whole. The rest of the people cast lots to determine who else would remain in the city to defend and build it up. One-tenth of the population was chosen to live in Jerusalem. The rest settled in the outlying towns and villages.

Verse 3 tells us that some of the priests, Levites, and temple servants lived in the towns of Judah. Likely, this was so that these towns could have religious leaders available to minister to the people there.

Verses 4-6 give us the list of individuals from Judah chosen to live in Jerusalem. In verses 7-9 is the list of descendants from Benjamin chosen by lot to live in Jerusalem. A number of priests chose to live in the city as well. The names of these priests are found in verses 10 and 11. These priests had associates who helped them in their work. The names of these associates are in verses 12-14. In total there were 1,192 male servants helping the priests in their duties. The Levites living in the city of Jerusalem totaled 284. The names of the heads of these households are found in verses 15-18. Another 172 gatekeepers watched the gates of the city (verse 19).

The other Israelites, priests, and Levites lived in the various towns of Judah on their ancestral properties. Temple servants living in the hill country of Ophel, Ziha, and Gishpa were given charge over those living in these various towns and villages.

Uzzi, a descendant of Asaph, was the chief officer of the Levites in Jerusalem. Asaph's descendants were in charge of the singers in the house of the Lord. Asaph wrote a number of Psalms (see Psalm 50; 73–83). The temple singers were directly responsible to the king who regulated their daily activities (verse 23).

In verse 24 we read that Pethahiah was the king's agent in charge of affairs related to the people. A list of villages where the people of Judah lived is found in verses 25–30. Seventeen cities or towns are mentioned here in these verses. Fifteen towns are listed in verses 31-36 where the descendants of Benjamin lived. Some Levites from Judah also lived with the tribe of Benjamin in their cities and villages.

We have here a clear record of how the people who returned from exile settled in the land. There was definite order in this matter. Of primary importance to the people was that the city of Jerusalem become a visible witness to the glory of God. Everyone was given access to a priest who could lead them in worship of the Lord God. As these people of God resettled in the land, they realized that the work of rebuilding had only just begun. There was much work ahead of them if they were to restore the nation of Israel to its former glory.

For Consideration:

• What sacrifices were made by those who lived in Jerusalem? What were their responsibilities to the city?

• What was the response of the people to those who volunteered to live in the city? What is our responsibility toward those who commit themselves to minister on our behalf?

- Notice that priests and Levites settled in the various towns and villages. What does this tell us about the importance of communities having a servant of God in their midst? Why is this important?

- Are there towns and villages in your region that do not have a minister of the gospel? What is the challenge of this passage in this regard?

For Prayer:

- The people of Israel commended those who were willing to live in the city of Jerusalem as their servants to protect the city and build it up. Who are your servants today? Take a moment to lift them up to the Lord.

- Are there towns and villages in your area that do not have a servant of the Lord to minister to them? Ask God to send a true servant to share the message of the gospel with them and to build them up in the faith.

- Ask the Lord to help you to be willing to make the necessary sacrifices for his kingdom. Thank the Lord for your spiritual leaders who have sacrificed much for the sake of the Lord.

23

A Ceremony at the Wall

Read Nehemiah 12:1–47

Chapter 12 begins with a list of priests and Levites who returned from exile. It should be noted here that there appears to have been different waves of returning exiles to the land of Jerusalem. In chapter 7 we read another listing of the first group that returned under Zerubbabel. The list in chapter 12 appears to be selective rather than exhaustive. Notice that Ezra is mentioned in verse 1. Verses 1–7 give us a list of the principle priests of that day.

Verses 8-11 list the names of the principle Levites. The Levites were assistants to the priests in the ministry of the temple. The Levites and their assistants mentioned in verse 8 were in charge of singing songs of thanksgiving to the Lord.

Verses 12-22 give us the names of the heads of the priestly families. Verses 22-23 tell us the location and time in which the heads of the Levite families were recorded.

The Levites mentioned in these verses had the responsibility for singing in the service of worship. We see from verse 24 that they sang opposite each other, with one section of musicians responding to another section in song, as David had prescribed.

The final list in this chapter is that of principle gatekeepers who were responsible for guarding the storerooms at the gates of the temple. Even gatekeepers were important in the work of the temple. No one was insignificant in the Lord's work. Each person had a specific role to fill in the temple, and every role was important and necessary.

In verse 27 we read about the dedication of the wall of Jerusalem. The wall had been completed and order had been restored in the city. It was time for the wall to be dedicated to the Lord. On the day of dedication, the Levites came to Jerusalem. Obviously, they came for the purpose of helping the people of God worship the Lord who had given them victory over their enemies. These Levites led the people in songs accompanied by the playing of cymbals, harps, and lyres. Singers were also brought from the surrounding areas for this special occasion. These singers had built villages for themselves around the city of Jerusalem (verse 29).

The priests and the Levites purified themselves according to the Law of Moses. Then they purified the people, the gates, and the wall to commit them to the Lord and to his service. Nehemiah had the leaders of Judah go on top of the wall with two large choirs. Each choir was to walk on the top of the wall in opposite directions. Ezra led one of the groups (verse 36). Nehemiah followed the second group in the opposite direction. As the choirs walked on the wall around the city, they sang praises to God and played their musical instruments to his honor. The city was surrounded by praise. As they walked on top of the wall, they declared publicly that the Lord God had given them victory. They declared him to be Lord in the city of Jerusalem.

The choirs then met in the temple and continued to sing and play their instruments in praise of the Lord God. Verse 43 tells us that they also offered sacrifices to the Lord that day with great joy. So great was the sound of rejoicing that the praise could be heard far away. This was a day for rejoicing in the Lord—they had returned to the land the Lord had promised them. Against all odds, they had achieved what their enemies said they could not achieve. They had persevered and overcome the enemy's obstacles.

During that time men were given charge of the storerooms where the contributions, firstfruits, and tithes of God's people would be kept until they were required for the service of the temple. God's people were to bring in their offerings to the storerooms, as the Law required.

From verse 45 we learn that the singers and the gatekeepers were also to perform the service of purification. That is to say, they too needed to be purified or set apart for the ministry to which the Lord had called them. They were to keep themselves pure in the work of the Lord. The offerings of God's people would also be used to provide for these individuals in their service for the Lord.

As we examine this chapter, we see the order that existed in the work of the Lord. Each person had a responsibility from the Lord. God's people were to be sure to provide for their temple workers so that the work of the temple would not suffer. The temple workers were to be pure and holy as they served the Lord their God. In all this the Lord was to be glorified. The temple was a place of music, worship, and celebration. Instruments and singers faithfully led in the worship of the Lord and the dedication of the wall. There was great joy and celebration that day. We too have much reason to celebrate the Lord. Our worship of him ought to be a celebration of victory. It ought to be a joyous experience. He is Lord and he has conquered all opposition. We share in that victory. This is reason for great rejoicing.

For Consideration:

- What role does music play in Old Testament worship? How important is music in the worship of our God today?

- Notice how God wanted ample provisions for the work of the temple. Does the work of God suffer in our day for lack of finances? What can you do to ease this?

- What significance was there in walking around the city wall, praising the Lord with music? Is it important that unbelievers recognize us as a people of praise? Explain.

- God's people had much to thank him for on the day they dedicated the walls of Jerusalem. What do you have to be thankful for today?

For Prayer:

- Ask the Lord to guide and provide for the leaders of your church. Ask him to show you how to use your finances.

- The temple servants needed to be purified as they began their task. Ask God to keep you pure and holy as his servant.

- What victories has the Lord God given you? Take a moment to praise and thank the Lord for those particular victories.

- Ask the Lord to help you never to be ashamed of praising him and declaring his glory and goodness to all those around you.

24

Cleaning House

Read Nehemiah 13:1–31

I t is quite likely that the events recorded in this final chapter of Nehemiah occurred some time after the renewal that had taken place in the land during his first visit. Nehemiah returned to his responsibilities in Persia under the king and after some time, came back to visit Jerusalem to see how things were going (see verses 6–7). During the time of his absence, the people of Jerusalem had allowed their situation to deteriorate. They had not persevered in their walk with God and in obedience to the binding agreement they had made with him. Nehemiah was very disappointed with what he saw on his return to Jerusalem. He took it on himself to do a spiritual house cleaning.

There are five situations mentioned in this chapter that give us an idea of what had happened over the course of time in the land of Israel. We will briefly examine each of these circumstances.

Removal of the Ammonites and Moabites from the Assembly (verses 1–3)

On one occasion as the Book of Moses was being read aloud, it was discovered that no Ammonite or Moabite was ever to be allowed into the assembly of God. The reason for this can be found in Numbers 22. There we read that when the children of Israel had camped on the Plains of Moab (after they had traveled for forty years through the wilderness and just before entering the Promised Land), the Moabites hired the prophet Balaam to curse Israel. God took this matter very seriously and judged Moab by forbidding them to enter his presence. The Lord refused to accept their worship. Ammon, Moab's neighbor, was also included in this judgment of God. Deuteronomy 23:3-4 tells us that both the Moabites and the Ammonites were forbidden access to the congregation of Israel because they refused to meet Israel with bread and water on their way out of Egypt and because they hired Balaam to curse Israel (Numbers 22).

This shows us just how dangerous a matter it is to hinder or seek to curse those whom God has blessed. In the Gospels the Lord Jesus warned: "But if anyone causes one of these little ones who believe in me to sin, it would be better for him to have a large millstone hung around his neck and to be drowned in the depths of the sea" (Matthew 18:6). Notice how seriously the Lord takes this matter of hindering or causing to sin those who believe in him. Our example is of utmost importance not only to the unbelieving world but also to believers around us. Here in the case before us, Moab hired a prophet to curse God's people.

Notice in verse 2 that God refused to allow Balaam to curse Israel. The Lord even turned the intended curse into a blessing. However, the people of Moab were still accountable to God for their evil intentions. God protected his children. He kept them from being destroyed by their enemies. Many evil forces will rise up against us, but God is our protector. He will use the efforts of our enemies to bring us blessing instead of cursing, and he will call our enemies to account for their actions against us.

Moab and Ammon had tried to stand in the way of what God wanted to do. They had tried to place a curse on God's people. We do not always understand what God is doing, but we must bless both his efforts and his chosen servants who are accomplishing his purposes. Moab refused to bless the children of God and paid a heavy price. May God give us a greater tolerance for our brothers and sisters.

When the people of Israel heard how God had forbidden any Moabite or Ammonite to be in the assembly of his people, they obeyed immediately. They removed the Ammonites and Moabites from their midst. They also separated from every person of foreign descent. No foreigner was permitted to enter the place of worship.

God desires absolute purity in service and worship. This is not to say that the doors of our church should be shut to unbelievers. What we do need to understand here is that in the ministry of the kingdom, God desires service from only those who know him. There are church leaders all over the world who do not even know the Lord. There are Sunday School teachers who are not living in a relationship with God but still teaching children. God desires that his children advance his kingdom. This is not the responsibility of the unbeliever. Israel had compromised in this area. Nehemiah had to deal with this upon his return to Jerusalem.

Removal of Tobiah (verses 4–9)

The second matter Nehemiah discovered related to the use of the storerooms in the temple. A priest by the name of Eliashib had been given charge of these storerooms. The storerooms were designed to hold the tithes, offerings, and firstfruits that were given by the people for the service of the Lord.

It seems that Eliashib was closely associated with Tobiah who was an Ammonite and a very bitter enemy of Nehemiah (2:10). Tobiah had done much to hinder the work on the wall surrounding the city (4:7-8), and he had also gained the favor of the Jewish nobles (6:17). Tobiah had also befriended Eliashib the priest who had provided Tobiah with a large storeroom in the temple of God. Tobiah had moved into this room and apparently was still living there when Nehemiah returned from Persia. When Nehemiah discovered what Eliashib the priest had done, he was greatly displeased. Nehemiah would have been angry for several different reasons. First, Tobiah was an Ammonite and should not have been allowed in the temple. Second, Tobiah had been one of the greatest enemies to the building of the wall of Jerusalem. Third, the storerooms were intended for the storage of tithes, offerings, and firstfruits. This room should have been filled with the gifts of God's people so that the work of the temple would not be hindered.

Nehemiah did not waste time here. He went into the storeroom and threw out all of Tobiah's household goods. He then ordered that the rooms be purified. Nehemiah had the temple equipment put back along with the grain offerings and the incense. He restored this space to its original purpose.

Restoring the Portions Assigned to the Levites (verses 10–14)

Nehemiah learned also that the portions allocated to the temple workers had not been given to them. God's people were not bringing in their offerings to the temple. This meant that temple workers had to work the land in order to have enough to live. The ministry of the temple suffered as a result.

Nehemiah rebuked the officials of the land because of this neglect. They were convicted of their sin and brought their tithes, grain, new wine, and oil offerings to the storerooms.

Nehemiah then put Shelemiah the priest, Zadok the scribe, and Pedaiah the Levite in charge of the storerooms. He also made Hanan an assistant. He did this because he knew them all to be trustworthy. These men were responsible for distributing the supplies to their brothers in the service of the temple.

Restoring the Sabbath (verses 15–22)

Nehemiah noticed that there were men in Judah who were treading the winepresses on the Sabbath. They were also bringing in grain and loading donkeys with grapes, figs, and other loads. The Sabbath was a commanded day of rest for Israel. The Book of Moses forbade anyone from doing work on that day. These individuals were totally ignoring the commandment of God.

Nehemiah also noticed that the merchants of Tyre who lived in Jerusalem were bringing in fish and other merchandise into the city and selling it on the Sabbath to the people of Israel. Seeing this, Nehemiah rebuked the nobles and reminded them of how their ancestors brought on themselves the wrath of God for doing the same thing. By ignoring the law of God, they were stirring up God's righteous anger.

When the next Sabbath evening came, Nehemiah ordered the city doors be closed and not opened until the Sabbath was over. He stationed men at the gates so that nothing could be brought into the city on that day. Once or twice, merchants came to sell their goods but were forced to spend the night outside the city. Nehemiah warned these merchants that if they came again on the Sabbath, he would personally lay hands on them. Therefore, these merchants decided to no longer come on the Sabbath.

The Sabbath Law was for the purpose of causing God's people to focus their attention on him. God's people were to learn how to trust him more. On this one day out of seven, they were to refrain from work. One year out of seven, they were not to plant their fields. God promised to take care of them in these times. By observing his commandments, God's people would know his blessing on their lives and recognize him as their provider.

Renouncing Foreign Marriages (verses 23–29)

Finally, Nehemiah noticed that there were men in Judah who had married foreign wives. He also noticed that half of their children spoke a foreign language and did not even know how to speak the language of Judah. This greatly disturbed Nehemiah. The language and faith of Israel was not being passed on to the next generation. This broke Nehemiah's heart.

Verse 25 tells us that Nehemiah rebuked these individuals and called down curses on them. He took some aside and beat them, pulling out their hair. In the culture of Israel, when a man shaved his hair, he was humbling himself. Nehemiah not only physically beat these individuals to punish them for their sin but he also pulled out their hair so that they would be put to shame for their evil. He then made them take an oath that they would never give their daughters or sons to marry any foreigner. Neither were they to take any foreign wives themselves. He reminded them that it was because of this very evil that Solomon fell into sin (1 Kings 11:4).

Notice in verse 28 that one of the sons of Joiada, son of Eliashib the high priest was son-in-law to Sanballat the Horonite. Sanballat was not only a foreigner but also worked with Tobiah to hinder the work of the wall. Nehemiah drove this young man from Israel. It grieved Nehemiah that even the priests had been guilty of permitting their children to intermarry with the foreigners of the land. As priests, they were under a special obligation before God to honor his covenant.

During his time in Jerusalem, Nehemiah restored obedience to God's laws. He removed the detestable practices from the land, purified the priests, and placed responsible people in spiritual leadership to assure that the Law of God would be observed.

What ought to strike us here is how quickly God's people wandered from the truth of his Word. Very rapidly, they began to compromise their faith. Soon the Law was twisted to suit their own preferences. Eventually, they turned completely from the Lord's commands.

We need to praise the Lord for men and women like Nehemiah who are concerned for the truth of God's Word. Nehemiah's heart was broken by the evil he saw in the land, and he refused to compromise. He would not accept anything but complete obedience to the Word of God. Nehemiah was not afraid of what others would think of him when he stood up for truth and discipline. All too many of us have become so blind to what is happening around us that we hardly notice evil in the land.

Could it be that we need to look deep inside our own hearts and take a spiritual inventory? Maybe our churches need to experience a spiritual cleansing. Nehemiah seems harsh in this passage. However this is how we need to be when it comes to sin in our midst. We need more people like Nehemiah who will not stand for sin but will root it out for the glory of God and the advancement of his kingdom, no matter the cost.

For Consideration:

• What do we learn here about the importance of purity among the people of God?

• Are there commands of God that you have trouble obeying? What are they?

- What do we learn from Nehemiah about the seriousness of sin?

- What foreign influences have come into our lives today?

- To what extent do you feel we have missed the blessing of God because we have failed to take sin as seriously as we should?

For Prayer:

- Ask the Lord to help you to pass on your faith to your own children. Take a moment to pray for them and their walk with God.

- Ask God to reveal anything in you that does not bring him honor and glory.

- Ask the Lord to give you a seriousness when it comes to sin. Ask him to help you to see sin as Nehemiah did.

- Ask God to give you strength to obey him, no matter the cost.

Esther

25

The Disobedience of Queen Vashti

Read Esther 1:1–22

The events of the book of Esther took place while God's people were in exile for their sin. The Persians were the dominant world power, having conquered the Babylonians. The reigning king of the time was King Xerxes. Verse 1 gives us an idea of the extent of his reign and power. He ruled over 127 provinces in a territory that stretched from India to the region of Ethiopia (Cush).

It was in the third year of his reign that Xerxes prepared a banquet for his nobles and officials. On that occasion the military leaders of Persia and Media and the princes of his provinces were present. The celebration was to last for six months (180 days). During that time, the king displayed the wealth of his kingdom to all who were present. Xerxes basked in his pride and arrogance. He openly displayed how rich and powerful he was. His officials would have been impressed by their king and his power. The show of power and wealth would have put a certain fear in the hearts of the nobles and officials. Their king was like a god to them.

When this lengthy celebration was over, Xerxes gave a great banquet lasting seven days in the enclosed garden of his palace. The banquet was open to everyone in the citadel at Susa, whether they were rich or poor. The garden was richly decorated for this celebration with hangings of white and blue linen. These hangings were fastened to marble pillars by white linen cords and silver rings (verse 6). The pavement was made from porphyry (a rock containing crystal formations and usually purple in color), marble, mother of pearl, and precious stones. Beautiful couches of gold and silver were scattered here and there on this pavement.

Wine was served in abundance in goblets of gold. Every goblet was a work of art in itself with no two goblets being the same. The king ordered that all guests be permitted to drink as much as they wished. We can only imagine the scene that day as guests drank all the wine they wanted. Drunkenness and all that comes with it would have been very noticeable that week. Queen Vashti, the wife of King Xerxes, offered a banquet for the women at the same time in a separate location.

By the seventh day, King Xerxes found his spirits high from wine. At that time he commanded seven eunuchs who served him to bring Queen Vashti before him wearing her royal crown. He wanted to show off her beauty to the drunken nobles who were present that day. When the servants told Vashti the king's command, Vashti refused to go.

While we are not told why Queen Vashti refused to obey the king's command, it would seem quite obvious that she was a respectable woman who did not wish to parade herself before a band of drunken men. This was not only beneath her dignity as a woman but also as a queen and example to other women in the community.

Vashti's refusal to obey the command of the king was an embarrassment to Xerxes. He was the most powerful king on the earth, but his own wife refused to bow to his command. This was especially embarrassing and dangerous because all the nobles were present that day to witness this challenge to his power. Xerxes consulted experts in the law and wise men who understood the times and asked them what should be done in such a case.

Memucan tells the king in verse 16 that Queen Vashti had wronged every noble and citizen of the king's provinces. He reminded King Xerxes that every woman in the nation would hear of the queen's conduct. They would follow her example and disrespect their husbands. Memucan advised the king to issue a royal decree and make it a law that Vashti never again be permitted to enter the presence of King Xerxes. Everything that belonged to Queen Vashti was to be taken from her, and her position was to be given to someone else. Memucan believed that by doing this, King Xerxes would make an example of Queen Vashti so that when the women of the nation saw what happened to her, they would learn to respect their husbands.

Those present at the banquet were pleased with the advice of Memucan. The king acted on Memucan's advice and stripped Vashti of her position. Dispatches were sent to all the provinces to share the news of Vashti's demise and to command that every man should be the ruler of his household.

There are a few points we need to consider in this chapter. First, this chapter calls us to examine the question of whether Vashti was right in what she did that day. Should Vashti have appeared before those drunken men just because her husband asked her to do so? Does headship in a family mean that the man can ask his wife to do whatever he wants and she is required to obey him? In this particular situation, Vashti was not willing to violate her moral principles. For her to display herself before these lustful and drunken nobles was not only beneath her dignity but would have violated a higher principle of morality.

In matters of preference, we need to be willing to submit to those who are over us. There are times, however, when we are asked to go against a higher moral or spiritual principle. In these cases we should be willing to disobey and suffer the consequences. The general principle, whether in marriage, work, or laws of the land, is that we respect and obey those who are over us. If I am at work, however, and my boss asks me to do something immoral or dishonest, I am obliged to obey God rather than my boss. It would seem to me that Vashti did what was right and proper in her situation. She was also willing to suffer the consequences of her disobedience.

Second, notice that sometimes even the righteous will suffer for doing what is right. We must be prepared for this. As servants of God, we will enter into conflict with the standards of this world. We need to be ready to suffer for doing what is right.

We will see the details of the final point as we move through this story of Esther. Queen Vashti's removal from her position would open the door for Esther to become queen. Through Esther God would save the nation of Israel from destruction. What we need to understand here is that God will use this event to accomplish his purposes for Israel. God's ways are quite strange at times. God blessed Vashti's decision. He needed to remove her so that his purposes could be accomplished. We will examine how this took place in the rest of this book.

For Consideration:

• What do we learn here about God's ways? How does God use the removal of Queen Vashti to accomplish his glory?

- What do we discover in this chapter about the spiritual climate of the land in the days of Xerxes?

- The Bible makes it quite clear that we are to be submissive to those who are in authority over us (see Romans 13). What should we do in a situation where the requests of those in authority over us enter into conflict with the clear moral and spiritual commands of God?

For Prayer:

- Ask the Lord to give you the grace to honor and obey those in authority over you.

- Ask God for strength and willingness to suffer for doing what is right.

- Take a moment to pray for those who are suffering today because they have done what was right.

26

In Search of a Queen

Read Esther 2:1–17

In the first chapter of this book, we saw how Queen Vashti was relieved of her position as queen. Her husband, King Xerxes, was not only under the influence of much wine at the time but was publicly embarrassed before the nobles who had come to his celebrations. When King Xerxes came to his senses, he realized what he had done. Verse 2 tells us that the king's personal attendants proposed that a search be made for a beautiful young virgin to get the king's mind off Queen Vashti. The hope was that this would cheer up the king.

The proposal was made that commissioners in every province in Xerxes' realm bring the most beautiful young virgins of their province to Susa to be part of the king's harem. They were to be placed under the care of the king's eunuch, a servant by the name of Hegai. He was to look after their beauty treatments and prepare them to meet the king. Given the size of the king's realm (from India to Ethiopia), this matter must have taken some time and required great effort.

The king's personal attendants proposed that the king examine each of these young virgins and select one of them to become queen in the place of Vashti. The king was quite delighted with this proposal and so he issued the decree.

In Susa lived a Jewish man by the name of Mordecai. He had been carried into exile when Nebuchadnezzar captured Jerusalem and brought back its choicest citizens to work for him as servants. Mordecai had a cousin named Hadassah. This girl had lost her father and mother and so he brought her up as his own child. Although Hadassah was a cousin to Mordecai, it is quite obvious that she was much younger.

Hadassah was also known as Esther. Hadassah was her Jewish name meaning "myrtle." Esther was her Persian name meaning "star." Esther, as she will be known throughout the rest of this book, was very beautiful. As such, she was a prime candidate for the king's harem. When the decree was issued, Esther and many other girls were brought to the citadel and put under the care of Hegai, the king's eunuch.

There was something particularly pleasing about Esther. She won Hegai's favor. Seeing her beauty and grace, he immediately began her beauty treatment. He also put her on a special diet. Esther was given seven maids to care for her needs and moved to the best place in the harem. Obviously, the hand of God was on her.

Many men and women of faith have seen the favor of God on them in such a way. Joseph experienced this in his time in Potiphar's house (Genesis 39:4). Nehemiah experienced the favor of God when he approached the king to ask for permission to return to Jerusalem (Nehemiah 2:5). The early church experienced this favor in the eyes of the unbelievers (Acts 2:47). Jesus experienced "favor with God and men" (Luke 2:52). When God wants to accomplish his purposes, he will sometimes give us favor with those to whom he is sending us. Certainly, this was the case with Esther.

When Esther had left for the king's harem, Mordecai had told her that she was not to reveal her nationality. To reveal that she was a Jew in that time would have put her at a disadvantage. The Jews were a conquered people. They were servants and did not have the same status as those of the region. We will discover in the course of this story that the fact that her nationality was hidden would work out to her advantage and ultimately bring great victory to the Jews. God had every detail worked out. Even the hiding of her identity would prove to be important.

Though Esther was no longer living in his home, Mordecai still was very concerned for her. Verse 11 tells us that every day he walked back and forth near the courtyard of the harem to find out how she was doing and what was happening to her. Obviously, he loved Esther very much and was deeply concerned for her situation.

Meanwhile, Hegai was busy preparing the girls to see the king. Before a girl could see the king, she had to undergo twelve months of beauty treatments. For six months she was treated with the oil of myrrh, very likely to soften the skin. In the remaining six months, special perfumes and cosmetics were applied to her skin.

When the day came for the young virgin to appear before the king, she was permitted to take anything she wanted from the harem. Likely, what this verse means is that she was given permission to take whatever jewelry or clothing she desired to make her impression on the king. The young virgin would go to the king in the evening and stay with him through the night. In the morning she would return to another part of the harem. After returning from the king, she would be placed under the direction of Shaashgaz, another one of the king's eunuchs, who was in charge of all the king's concubines. These women were to remain under the care of Shaashgaz and would not see the king again unless he called for them by name. Adam Clarke, in his comments on Esther 2:14, tells us that after this the concubine would never be given in marriage to another man. (*Adam Clarke's Commentary on the Bible*). While they would be well cared for, these women were to be reserved for the king alone but only permitted to enter his presence when called for by name.

When Esther's turn came to see the king, she listened carefully to the advice of Hegai. She was taken to see the king in the tenth month of the seventh year of Xerxes' reign. When the king met Esther, he was attracted to her. She won his special favor and approval. He was pleased to put the royal crown on her head so that she became queen in the place of Vashti.

In all of this, we see the work of a sovereign God. Vashti was removed from her position so that Esther could take her place. While the whole empire was involved in this process, God was over all. He worked out all the events to accomplish his purposes. Esther became the queen of the most powerful nation on the earth. The hand of God was moving by granting favor to Esther. She willingly stepped out in that favor and passed through the doors God was opening for her. God was setting up the scene to accomplish the salvation of his people. Even before his people were in need, God prepared a solution. What a wonderful thought this is. Through the prophet Isaiah, God said: "Before they call I will answer; while they are still speaking I will hear" (Isaiah 65:24).

God knows what our needs will be even before we have those needs. He has already prepared the solutions to our future problems. Our prayers are already answered in the mind of God. The Lord is arranging circumstances and situations so that his answers can become realities. How we need to thank the Lord that he cares for us in this way.

For Consideration:

- How does God prepare the way for Esther to accomplish his purposes? What encouragement do you take from this in your own life and ministry?

- Who does God use to accomplish his purpose of making Esther the queen? Are these people aware that they are the instruments of God to bring salvation to his people? What does this tell us about God?

- What encouragement do you find in the fact that the Lord has prepared answers to the problems of his people even before there is any evidence of these problems?

For Prayer:

- Thank the Lord that he is a sovereign God who works out all things according to his purposes.

- Thank the Lord that he knows what you need before you even have the need. Thank him that he is working out the solution to the problems you have not yet faced.

- Ask God to give you favor with those who are between you and the accomplishing of his purpose for your life.

27

Haman and Mordecai

Read Esther 2:18–3:15

By the grace of God, Esther had become queen in the land of Persia. Unknown to her and the Jews of that day, God was preparing the scene for a terrible declaration that would threaten to exterminate them as a people in the land of Persia.

In verse 18 King Xerxes prepared a great banquet in honor of his new wife. He assembled his nobles and officials and proclaimed a holiday throughout the provinces of his land. Gifts were given with liberality. Xerxes seems to have been a man of great extravagance.

During the time of the celebrations, Mordecai was sitting outside the king's gate. As he sat there, two of the kings officers who guarded the gate became very angry and planned to kill King Xerxes. Mordecai heard about the plot and told Queen Esther who reported it to Xerxes and gave the credit to Mordecai. When the report was investigated and discovered to be true, the two officials were hanged.

The incident was recorded in the records in the presence of the king. At that time nothing was done to reward Mordecai, but all this was in God's hand. The time would come when Mordecai would be rewarded—but not yet. God's timing is not like ours.

After this event King Xerxes honored a man by the name of Haman and gave him a position that was higher than any of the other nobles. The command of the king was that everyone should honor Haman. Wherever he went, people would kneel down and pay their respects to him. Mordecai, however, refused to pay him honor.

We may legitimately ask why Mordecai refused to bow down to Haman. The answer may be found in the command the king gave to his people concerning Haman. Verse 2 tells us that the king commanded his people to "honor" Haman. The Hebrew word here is *shachah*, which can mean "to worship or reverence." It is quite likely that Haman was expecting to be worshiped as a god. If this was the case, the reason why Mordecai refused to bow down was that, as a Jew, Mordecai would only bow the knee in worship of the God of Israel. Mordecai willingly risked his life to be obedient to the command of the Lord God of Israel.

The refusal of Mordecai to bow down and worship Haman perplexed the royal officials at the king's gate. They asked Mordecai why he refused to obey the command of the king and thus risk his life. Each day they tried to persuade him to bow down before Haman, but Mordecai continually refused.

Verse 4 tells us that Mordecai revealed to the royal officials that he was a Jew. This is important. Could it be that the reason why Mordecai was compelled to reveal this fact was because he was explaining to the officials that, as a Jew, it was against his faith to bow down in worship to anyone but the one true God?

On hearing this explanation, the officials went to Haman and told him what Mordecai had said. It may be that the officials wondered if leniency would be given to Mordecai because of his faith. Haman was very angry, however, when he heard that Mordecai refused kneel down in worship despite repeated efforts of the officials to convince him to do so. When Haman heard that Mordecai was a Jew, he decided to kill all the Jews in the Persian Empire. This decision was made partly because of Mordecai, but we should not see this as the only reason for Haman's decision. Haman hated all Jews because he saw them as an obstacle to his own aspirations of being worshiped as a god. Because Jews were forbidden to worship any God but the Lord, they stood in the way of Haman's ambitions of being worshiped throughout the Persian Empire.

It should also be noted here that Haman was an Agagite (3:1). Agag was an Amalekite king in the days when Saul was king of Israel (1 Samuel 15). After an attack on the Amalekites, King Saul spared Agag. This angered God who had commanded Saul to utterly destroy these peoples. God sent his prophet Samuel to confront Saul about this matter. Samuel became the instrument of divine judgment and killed Agag with the sword. The Amalekites continued to be an enemy of Israel (1 Samuel 30). Haman would have been aware of this history and it may have contributed to his anger toward Israel.

With the decision fixed in his mind, Haman needed only to decide when and how he should execute his plan to exterminate the Jews. To determine this he cast the *pur*. This means that Haman cast "lots." We are not told how this was done. It could be that he rolled a dice or did something of this nature to fix the month when his evil plan was to be carried out. Casting the *pur* may even have been part of a religious ceremony.

When the month was fixed, Haman went to King Xerxes and revealed his plan. Haman told the king of a people whose customs were different from theirs. He told Xerxes of how the Jews refused to obey the king's laws. This might lead us to believe that Mordecai was not the only one who refused to bow down to Haman. Haman advised the king that it would be in his interest to destroy these people.

Haman hid his hate of Mordecai in the guise of loyalty to the king. Haman even offered to put ten thousand talents of silver into the royal treasury for the men who would carry out this plan and proposed that a decree be issued to this effect.

Xerxes took his signet ring from his finger and gave it to Haman. The ring was a symbol of authority. It was used to stamp official documents. When the king gave his ring to Haman, he was in effect giving him full authority to carry out the evil plot. Notice in verse 11 that King Xerxes placed full confidence in Haman. He told him to keep his money but to do whatever he felt was necessary with the Jews.

Very little time was wasted in this matter. On the thirteenth day of that same month secretaries were assembled for the purpose of writing out the king's decree in the various languages of the people. The orders were then sealed with the king's signet ring and made official.

Messengers were sent to all the king's provinces with the order to annihilate all Jews. No Jews were to be spared. Young, old, women, and little children were to be killed. This was to happen in a single day, the thirteenth day of the twelfth month. Everyone in the kingdom was to be ready to perform this terrible deed on that day and then to plunder all the possessions of the murdered Jews.

Having issued his decree, Haman and the king sat down to drink. The city of Susa, however, was confused by this horrible command. Behind it was a very evil, jealous, and proud mind. Controlling all this evil, however, was a sovereign God who knew what would happen. Even then, God was working out his plan to defend his people. While the king and Haman drank together in celebration, God prepared the defeat of all their plans.

For Consideration:

- What do we learn here about the courage of Mordecai?

- Have you ever found yourself in a situation where you were tempted to hide or compromise your faith? What challenge does Mordecai bring to us?

- Have you ever found yourself in a situation where you felt that things were completely out of control and all hope was lost? What encouragement do you find here in the fact that though outwardly things appear to be very terrible, God is still working behind the scenes?

For Prayer:

- Ask the Lord to give you courage to stand firm in your walk with him.

- Thank the Lord that he is a sovereign God who controls the future.

- Thank God that no matter how difficult things appear, in him there is always hope.

28

If I Perish, I Perish

Read Esther 4:1–17

The plan to exterminate the Jews had been decreed. Messengers traveled to the far corners of the Persian Empire to issue the order that on a certain day all citizens were to rise up to kill the Jews and plunder their possessions.

The news of this plot reached Mordecai. When he learned of Haman's plan, he tore off his clothes, put on sackcloth and ashes as a sign of mourning, and went out into the city, wailing bitterly. The burden would have been particularly great for Mordecai because he understood that it was because of his refusal to bow down to Haman that this evil had come on them as a nation. He may have wondered why the Lord would have permitted this to happen when he had been faithful in keeping the Lord's commandments. What made matters worse was that he could only go as far as the king's gate because no one who was dressed in sackcloth and ashes was allowed to enter. This meant that he did not have access either to the king to petition him for mercy or to Esther who could have seen the king on his behalf.

There was a similar response everywhere the decree was read. The Jews in all the provinces mourned, fasted, wept, and wore sackcloth and ashes. God's people turned to him in this time of trouble. They had nowhere to turn but to the Lord, so they fasted and sought his mercy.

It was Esther's maids and eunuchs who came and told her about Mordecai. On learning that Mordecai was dressed in sackcloth, Esther sent clothes for him to put on. Obviously, she did not know what was troubling Mordecai, and he refused the clothes.

Esther understood that something very serious was disturbing Mordecai. She called Hathach, one of the eunuchs assigned to attend to her, and commanded him to speak to Mordecai to find out what was worrying him. Hathach did as he was commanded and learned about the plot to kill the Jews. Mordecai gave Hathach a copy of the decree for the annihilation of the Jews. Through Hathach, Mordecai pleaded with Esther to approach the king to plead for mercy and beg him to save her people. We need to see here that while Mordecai did not have direct access to Esther now that she was queen, God opened a door for him to speak to her through her servant Hathach.

When Esther received the report from Hathach, she sent him back to remind Mordecai that the custom of the royal court stated that no man or woman was ever permitted to approach the king in his inner court without first being summoned. Anyone who did so would be put to death unless, at that moment, the king extended his scepter to them and spared their life. Esther reminded Mordecai that she had not been called to see the king and to see him without being summoned would be to risk her life.

Esther is not sure what she was to do. She no doubt grieved for her people and for Mordecai, but if the king was not pleased with her, she would be killed and not be of any benefit to her people. When Mordecai heard what Esther had to say, he told her that she would not be spared just because she was in the king's house. Mordecai was telling her that her life was also in danger. Once it was discovered that she was a Jew, the king would be forced to kill her to obey his own decree. Whether or not she approached the king, her life was in danger. Mordecai went on to reminded Esther that if she remained silent at this time, God would raise up deliverance from another source, but she and her household would perish. He reminded her that it might have been for this very purpose that she was queen.

Mordecai's response was very wise. There are several things we should notice in his response. First, notice that Mordecai reminded Esther that she was in danger herself. It may be that Esther had become comfortable in her situation. She was living with a false sense of security. She believed that because she was queen, she would be spared. Mordecai made her realize that this was not the case. She was in danger whether she saw it or not. Esther wasn't sure if she should risk her life. Mordecai reminded her that if she did not do something, she would perish even though she was queen.

Many people live today with a false security. They believe that because they go to church or because they accepted Jesus as their Savior, they will not have to answer to God for their actions. The reality of the matter is that we will all have to answer to God on that final day of judgment.

Second, notice that Mordecai believed in deliverance. He realized that the situation looked very dismal. He did not know how the Lord was going to set his people free from this evil plot, but he spoke of God's deliverance for his people. Mordecai believed that Esther could be the answer to this problem. He told her that if she did not do something, God would raise up someone else to be the deliverer.

God can use anyone to accomplish his purposes. Mordecai believed that Esther was the instrument of God, but he did not place his faith in her. It was God who would deliver, not Esther. If she refused to take on the responsibility, God would find someone else.

God is preparing each one of us for a particular ministry. The circumstances he has put you through and the trials you have had to bear are all preparation for that ministry. Not everyone accepts God's calling, however. Some people are disobedient. Some are fearful. If we do not follow God's call, we will suffer great loss. We will not see the fruit that God intended for our lives. We will suffer spiritually. God's purposes will not be hindered, however. He is fully able to use someone else to accomplish those purposes.

Mordecai reminded Esther of God's sovereign purposes. He challenged her to take a look at what the Lord had done over the last while. He challenged her to ask the questions: Why has God placed me in this palace? Why has he given me this position? Mordecai somehow believed that God had given Esther this place of honor so that she could be his instrument in this hour of need. As much as he loved Esther, Mordecai challenged her to take the risk and go to the king.

Mordecai's words caused Esther to think. She sent word to Mordecai to gather all the Jews of Susa and ask them to fast three days for her. She and her maids would do the same. After three days she would risk her life and go to the king, even though it was against the law. In verse 16 she resigned herself to the will of God: "If I perish, I perish," she said. Encouraged by this, Mordecai gathered the Jews of Susa together and called them to pray and fast for three days.

God needed to bring Esther to the point where she was willing to risk everything. This is a place where we all need to be in our relationship with God. Are we willing to risk everything to accomplish what God has called us to do? It was relatively easy for Esther when God called her to be queen and live in the lap of luxury. But then God called her to be willing to lay aside all of that and risk her life for him. Would we be willing to go this far for the sake of the Lord and his kingdom?

For Consideration:

- Do bad things happen to good people? What evidence is there here to support your answer?

- Esther may have had a false sense of security in this chapter. What false securities might we cling to today?

- What do we learn here about the sovereignty of God in working out the circumstances of life? Is there evidence in your life of how God prepared you for a particular ministry or challenge? Explain.

- How important is it that we come to the place where we are willing to risk everything for the Lord?

For Prayer:

- Ask the Lord to bring you to the point of laying down everything for him.

- Thank the Lord that he is a sovereign God who works out his purposes and plans for our lives.

- Ask the Lord to make you willing to follow him not only in the easy times but also in the difficult times.

29

A Banquet and a Gallows

Read Esther 5:1–14

The Jews of Susa had fasted and prayed for three days at the invitation of Queen Esther. On the third day, she approached the king to seek his favor and mercy for her people. Though approaching the king without invitation could mean death, Esther willingly took the risk for the sake of her people.

On the third day, Esther dressed in her royal robes and stood in the inner court of the palace in front of the king's hall. The king was sitting on his throne facing the entrance when she walked in. This was the moment of truth. Would the king have mercy and extend his scepter or would he order that she be killed for defying the law of the court?

When the king saw Esther, he was pleased with her. To show his favor, he extended his scepter. Esther approached and touched the tip of the scepter. It appears that touching the tip of the scepter was a means of recognizing, receiving, and expressing gratitude for the king's favor and mercy.

When the formalities were over, King Xerxes asked Esther what she wanted. He offered her up to half his kingdom. Obviously, he understood that she would not willingly defy the law of the court without reason.

While Esther could have made her requests known at that time to the king, she chose to ask him to come to a great banquet she was preparing for him. She also invited Haman. King Xerxes, from what we have seen of him in the first part of this book, seemed to enjoy feasting and celebrating. He was quite delighted to accept the invitation and ordered that Haman be brought at once so they could attend the banquet Esther had prepared for them.

It is uncertain why Esther did not immediately ask the king to spare the lives of her people. Maybe she felt she needed to prepare him for this request. Maybe the timing was not right. It seems to be clear that she did not have the freedom from the Lord to ask the king at this time. She waited for the right moment. The right words spoken at the wrong time will not produce the desired result. As representatives of the Lord, we need to know what the Lord would have us to speak. It is just as important, however, for us to wait for the Lord's timing in speaking that word.

As the king drank wine at Esther's banquet, he again asked her what was on her mind and what he could give her. Again, he promised her up to half his kingdom. For the second time, Esther asked him to return the next day with Haman for another banquet. She promised to give him her request at that time.

As Haman left the banquet that evening, he was very happy. As he passed the king's gate, however, he saw Mordecai sitting there. He noticed that Mordecai refused to bow down to him, and this made him very angry. Verse 10 tells us that Haman restrained himself and went home. Haman could have done something right then to have

Mordecai punished, but God did not permit this to happen. God protected Mordecai on this occasion.

When he returned home that evening, Haman called his friends and wife together. He boasted to them about his vast wealth, his many sons, and all the ways in which the king had honored him above every other noble in the land. He told them of how Esther had invited him alone to the banquet she had prepared for the king and how she had invited him to return the next day. Haman felt important. He saw himself as the most important man in the Persian Empire, next to the king himself.

Haman then told his friends and wife that all this gave him no satisfaction as long as Mordecai refused to bow to him and recognize his authority and dignity. Mordecai was a thorn in his side. Haman's wife Zeresh and his friends suggested that Haman build a gallows seventy-five feet high (twenty-three meters). The idea was to humiliate Mordecai. A gallows this high would be clearly visible. People would be able to see him hanging from this gallows all over the city. Haman liked the idea but did not have the right to pass the death sentence. He decided, therefore, to ask the king in the morning for permission to have Mordecai hung from these gallows for his refusal to honor and respect him as the king's representative. Haman immediately ordered that the gallows be built, expecting a positive response from the king.

As for Mordecai, problems seemed to be increasing. Time was running out for all the Jews, and his life was immediately at stake. If Haman had his way, Mordecai had only one more day to live. God's timing is not the same as ours. What appeared to be the end of all hope was in reality the beginning of God's wonderful plan of deliverance.

There are several principles we need to see in this passage. First, notice the hand of God on the lives of his people. We see this in the way God answered the prayers of his people and gave Esther favor in the eyes of the king. We also see his favor on Mordecai as he kept him from Haman's anger at the king's gate. God does answer prayer. On the surface, we see the evil schemes of individuals to destroy the people of God. Behind the scenes, however, the Spirit of God is moving in a powerful way to bring victory to his people. We are easily deceived by the outward appearance. God works quietly behind the scenes to accomplish his purpose.

Second, notice the importance of waiting on God's timing. Esther did not immediately bring her request to the king. It was not God's time. Haman needed to build a gallows. Those gallows would be proof to the king of his evil intentions. We will also discover in the next chapter that the king himself needed to be prepared for Esther's request. There is a right time for everything. Only when Haman and the king had been properly prepared by God would Esther be permitted to share her request. Esther needed to be in tune with God's timing.

When he was forty years of age, Moses had a burden for his people (Acts 7:23). He wanted his people to see him as their deliverer (Acts 7:25). While it was the will of God to use Moses to deliver his people, the timing was not right. Moses was not ready to be used. God sent him into the wilderness for forty years. Only when he was eighty years of age did God permit Moses to return to Egypt for the purpose of delivering his people.

Timing is important. The right word or the right action at the wrong time will not accomplish the purpose of God. The Lord may burden us and place a message on our heart but he also intends for us to wait for his timing. Behind the scenes, God is working to prepare the hearts and lives of those to whom that message is intended. We must be in tune with God in this matter.

For Consideration:

- In this chapter we see how the enemies of God's people plotted against them. At that same time, however, we see the hand of God at work. What evidence is there that God was at work in the lives of his people in this chapter?

- Take a moment to consider the ways in which God is at work in your life today.

- Why is timing important in the ministry of the kingdom of God?

- Have you ever found yourself so anxious to accomplish the work of God that you did not wait for him? What was the result?

- How can you know when the timing of God is right? Do you have personal examples of bad timing? What about examples of good timing?

For Prayer:

- Ask God to help you to wait for his timing in your ministry and decisions.

- Thank the Lord that he does answer prayers. Thank him that he does this despite all the efforts of the enemy to defeat us.

- Thank the Lord that he extends his hand of favor to us, as the king did for Esther. Thank him for the privilege of being a chosen servant in whom he delights.

- Ask the Lord to forgive you for the times you failed to trust his purposes and looked more on the outward appearance of a situation. Ask him to give you faith to trust him even when things don't appear to be going in the direction you had hoped.

30

A Reward in Its Proper Time

Read Esther 6:1–14

In the last meditation, we saw how Esther invited the king and Haman to a banquet in their honor. At that time the king asked Esther for the second time what he could do for her, but Esther was not prepared to share her request with the king. Instead, she asked him to return to a second banquet she was preparing for him and Haman. At that time she would give him her answer.

What is important for us to understand is how God is working behind the scenes to accomplish his purpose. As Esther waited for the right moment to ask the king to save her people, Haman moved forward in his plan to kill Mordecai. The gallows were being prepared to hang Mordecai, but this would ultimately work against Haman.

While Haman was preparing the gallows for Mordecai, God was also working in the king's life. That evening the king could not sleep. He ordered that the book of the chronicles of his reign be brought to him. As he read the account of his reign, the king's attention was drawn to an incident recorded in the chronicle about Mordecai who had saved his life by exposing an assassination plot. There was no record in the chronicle of any honor or recognition given Mordecai for exposing this plot. The king asked his servants what had been done to recognize Mordecai for his actions. His attendants assured him that Mordecai had never been recognized or honored for his deed.

Again, we see the importance of God's timing in all matters. As the king thought about what he needed to do for Mordecai, Haman appeared in the court. He had come at that precise moment to ask the king for permission to hang Mordecai from the gallows he had prepared. The king asked that Haman be brought before him. When Haman approached, the king asked, "What should be done for the man the king delights to honor?" (verse 6).

Haman could never have imagined that the king was speaking about Mordecai when he asked this question. Haman thought the king was speaking about him. Thinking of himself, Haman told the king that he should dress the person he wanted to honor in one of his own royal robes and place him on a horse the king himself had ridden. Haman then suggested that this honored person should be led through the streets of the city by one of the king's most noble princes, proclaiming, "This is what is done for the man the king delights to honor!" (verse 9).

The matter of wearing one of the king's royal robes and riding a horse the king had ridden was a very great honor. In that day even the king's wives could not approach him without special invitation. In reality, the king was saying that the person whom he privileged in this way was equally worthy of the people's honor.

The king liked Haman's idea and suggested that Haman lead the horse through the city with Mordecai seated on it. We can only imagine how devastating this must have been for Haman. He had come to ask for Mordecai's death, but instead he was ordered to honor Mordecai as no other man had been honored. To parade Mordecai through the city in this regal way would have been humiliating for Haman. Added to this was the fact that the gallows were even now being built to hang the man the king wanted to honor. This would not go well with the king. It would set Haman against the king because it would be found out that he planned to kill the man who had saved the king's life.

After he had paraded Mordecai through the city in this way, Haman returned home filled with grief. He told his wife and friends what had happened that day. His advisers made a very interesting observation. They told him that because Mordecai was of Jewish origin, he could not stand against him. Haman's ruin was sure.

There may be various reasons why Haman's advisers made this statement. It may have been because they had heard about the God of the Jews. He was a powerful God who fought for his people. Haman was setting himself up against the God of the Jews and, therefore, could not possibly succeed. Beyond this, however, was the fact that Mordecai had just been honored above Haman. Mordecai had achieved a very powerful position in the land. As a Jew, he would not sit by and watch Haman destroy his people. Haman's plot to kill the Jews would be exposed and he would be seen as a traitor to the king.

Haman was still speaking to his advisors about this matter when the king's eunuchs came to escort him to the banquet Esther had prepared. When he went this time, however, Haman was not quite so proud. There would have been fear in his heart. Overnight his position before the king had changed. The proud boasts of Haman were stopped in an instant.

God works in his own time. As Esther delayed, God worked. Soon the time would be perfect for her to ask the king to save her people from the hands of Haman. Two days before, the response of the king would have been very different. Now, his heart was prepared to give Esther her request. Many times we do not see what God is doing. In an instant, everything can change. The answer to the problem the Jews were experiencing came overnight. One moment they were in despair; the next moment they were rejoicing in victory. Victory is often much quicker than we could ever imagine.

For Consideration:

* Why is timing so important in the work of the kingdom of God?

* What is God doing behind the scenes in this passage? Could it be that God is working out the solution to the problem you are facing today?

* Are you facing a trial that seems to be overwhelming right now? What does this passage tell us about how close that victory could be?

* What evidence is there that the time was right for Esther to share her request?

For Prayer:

* Thank the Lord that he is a God who answers prayer.

* Ask that Lord to forgive you for the times when you have doubted his plan and purpose.

* Thank the Lord that he is always working for our good. Praise him that he has already heard your request and is even now working on the solution.

- Ask God to help you to know how to wait on him and his timing.

- Ask the Lord to forgive you for the times you have stepped out too quickly and taken matters into your own hands.

31

The Reversal of Haman's Plot

Read Esther 7:1–8:17

This was the second banquet that Esther had prepared for the king and Haman. Haman came to this second banquet, however, with a heavy heart. The king had just honored Mordecai whom Haman had intended to hang. Haman's advisers had told him that now that Mordecai had such influence, his plot to kill the Jews could not succeed.

As the king and Haman dined with Esther, things would get worse for Haman. Unknown to him, Esther and Mordecai were related. In addition, Haman did not know that Esther was a Jew. As they were drinking wine that day, the king asked Esther for the third time: "Queen Esther, what is your petition? It will be given you. What is your request? Even up to half the kingdom, it will be granted" (7:2).

This time Esther would give the king her answer. Everything had been prepared. To the shock of the king that evening, Esther asked him to save her life and to spare her people. She told the king that she and her people had been sold to destruction, slaughter, and annihilation. She told him that if they had merely been sold as slaves, she would not have bothered him, but she could not bear to see the annihilation of her people.

We can only imagine the response of Haman as he sat there at that banquet table. Fear and terror would have overcome him. He had not known that Esther was of Jewish nationality. What she was telling the king surely struck dread in Haman's heart.

King Xerxes was very obviously disturbed by this request. He asked Esther who would dare to do such a thing. Esther pointed to Haman. Haman was speechless. His heart was filled with terror as he looked at the king.

The king left the banquet in a rage and went out into the palace garden. At that point, King Xerxes must have felt betrayed. Haman had been his trusted servant. He had lifted him up above all other servants in the land. He had trusted him implicitly. When he had come to ask permission to deal with a people whom he said were in opposition to the king's reign, Xerxes had simply trusted him. Very likely, as he walked in his garden, the king considered his options.

When the king left the banquet, Haman stayed behind with Esther. He knew that his life was in danger. Esther was reclining on a couch in the banquet hall. Just as the king returned from the garden, he saw Haman falling on the couch where Esther reclined. The king was not pleased. He accused Haman of molesting the queen. Servants immediately covered Haman's face. The covering of Haman's face was typical of what would happen to the condemned criminal. It was a symbolic way of saying that the individual was no longer worthy to look on the face of the king. The covering of Haman's face was his sentence of death.

It was one of the king's eunuchs, a man by the name of Harbona, who told the king that Haman had ordered the construction of the seventy-five-foot gallows for the purpose of hanging Mordecai. This was an even greater insult to the king. Just that day the king had honored Mordecai for saving his life. Haman had been planning to hang the man who had saved the king.

The king ordered that Haman be hung on the gallows he had prepared for Mordecai. The enemy of God's people was defeated, but there was still much to do to save the lives of the Jews. Haman's order had already gone out, and it could not be changed. God's people were still in serious danger of annihilation.

That very same day, King Xerxes gave Queen Esther Haman's estate. This estate would have been worth a considerable fortune, as Haman was the highest ranking official in the kingdom.

Esther told the king that she was related to Mordecai. When the king heard this, he commanded that Mordecai be brought into his presence. That day the king took off his signet ring, the symbol of his authority that he had reclaimed from Haman, and gave it to Mordecai. Esther appointed Mordecai to be in charge of Haman's estate. Everything that belonged to Haman was given to Esther and Mordecai. God took Haman's life and wealth and gave it to his own people. God spoiled the enemy's plan and stripped him of his power.

That day Esther pleaded with the king to put an end to the evil plot of Haman. King Xerxes listened to Esther and extended his gold scepter to her as a sign of his favor. Esther asked the king to write an order overruling the command of Haman. The king could not do this because Haman's decree was official. It had been stamped with the king's signet ring and could not be changed. But King Xerxes did give Esther and Mordecai permission to write a different decree—this one on behalf of the Jews. The king told them to write it as seemed best to them and to seal it with the king's own signet ring, making it official and irrevocable (verse 8). The challenge was for Esther and Mordecai to write a decree that would protect the Jews but not change what Haman had decreed.

In verse 9 the royal secretaries were summoned. A decree was drafted for the governors and nobles of the 127 provinces stretching from India to Ethiopia. This decree was translated into the languages of all the provinces so all could understand. It was written in the name of King Xerxes and sealed with his signet ring. Couriers were sent on fast horses to each of the provinces to bring the king's decree to the governors and nobles.

The decree granted the Jews in every city the right to defend themselves. They could destroy, kill, or annihilate any armed force of any nationality or province that might attack them, their women, or their children. The Jews were also given the right to plunder the property of their enemies. This decree was issued as law in every province. It enabled the Jews to legally defend themselves. Mordecai's wisdom is seen in this decree. Knowing that he could not change the decree of Haman, Mordecai discouraged the enemies of God's people from attacking.

Mordecai left the presence of the king dressed in royal robes and a large gold crown. The city of Susa celebrated his promotion. Especially for the Jews, this was a day of great joy, feasting, and praise. God had been faithful. Haman's evil plot had been reversed.

What is of great interest to us here is that verse 17 tells us that many people from the various provinces became Jews because the fear of God had seized them. God protected and strengthened his people and also added to their number.

Earlier, Mordecai had given Esther to God and to his will for her life. Mordecai had given her to be the wife of the king, and this was not without personal sacrifice. During that time he was not able to see Esther. But God had blessed Esther and Mordecai and brought them back together. Mordecai had waited patiently and obediently, and God had blessed his faith. Mordecai and Esther served the Lord together. God does reward faithful sacrifice.

What a blessing it is to know that no weapon forged against us will prevail (Isaiah 54:17). God will strip our enemies of their swords. God is the protector of his people. There were many times when Israel did not understand the purpose and plan of God. Their enemies seemed to prevail, but God would not let his people be destroyed. He cared too much for them. He is the same God today. He cares for us and will protect us. As we wait for the Lord and trust in him, we too will see this same victory in his time.

For Consideration:

- Once again, we see the importance of the Lord's timing in this passage. How is this timing evident in this section?

- What weapons has the enemy been using against you? What encouragement do you receive from this passage?

- What do we learn here about how God rewards those who are faithful to him?

- What particular struggle are you facing today? What are the promises of God for you here?

For Prayer:

- Thank the Lord that he is your protector.

- Ask the Lord to help you to live like Esther and Mordecai in absolute obedience to his Word, purpose, and timing.

- Thank the Lord that he is able to turn the enemy's sword against him.

- Take a moment to consider the way the Lord has guided and blessed you. Thank him for those blessings.

32

Purim: A Celebration of Victory

Read Esther 9:1–10:3

Things had radically changed for the people of God. In just a short while, the Lord had turned the tables on Haman. A decree had gone out in the land that the people of God were to take up arms to defend themselves against any enemy that might attack them.

On the day of the attack, the Jews assembled in all the provinces of King Xerxes to defend themselves. God gave the Jews victory that day. When their enemies came to fight, the Jews defeated them. Even the nobles, governors, and satraps of the various provinces chose to side with the Jews because they feared Mordecai who had become very important in the land. He held a prominent position at the palace and his reputation had quickly spread throughout the empire.

Verse 5 tells us that on the day of the attack, the Jews struck down their enemies with the sword. In the citadel of Susa alone, the Jews killed five hundred men. Among them were ten sons of Haman. Though they were permitted by law to plunder their enemies, the Jews refused to do so.

When the king heard how many men were slain in Susa that day, he was concerned. He questioned Esther about what had happened in the rest of his kingdom. Though the numbers concerned him, Esther still found favor in his eyes. Despite the loss of lives that day, the king still gave Esther full permission to carry out her plan. When Esther asked permission for the Jews to carry out the edict for one more day as well as permission to hang the ten sons of Haman on the gallows, the king readily agreed. Esther and Mordecai were intent on wiping out their enemies.

In all of this, we see the tremendous favor of the Lord on the Jews. From that point on, there could have been no doubt in the minds of the citizens of the Persian Empire that King Xerxes was protecting the Jews and saw them as his friends. With Queen Esther being of Jewish nationality and Mordecai in such a high position in government, people would have hesitated before speaking out against the Jews.

The next day, as the king had commanded, the Jews in Susa gathered again and put to death another three hundred men, for a total of eight hundred dead in Susa. In other provinces another seventy-five thousand enemies lay dead at the hands of the Jews. On the fourteenth day of the month, the Jews of the provinces celebrated their victory. In Susa, because they were given permission to fight one more day, they celebrated their victory on the fifteenth day of the month.

Mordecai recorded these events and wrote letters to the Jews in various provinces to have them remember the fourteenth and fifteenth days of the month of Adar. Every year in remembrance of God's great mercy and grace, the Jews were to celebrate this victory over the enemy. The Jews were to celebrate the occasion by feasting, joyous celebration, and giving gifts to one another and to the poor.

The celebration is known as Purim. The name comes from the word *pur*. In Esther 3:7 Haman had decided when he would carry out his evil plot by casting the *pur*. To cast the *pur* meant to cast "lots." The lot may have been some form of dice that were cast to determine the will of the gods. Purim is the celebration of how the Lord overruled the decision made by the *pur*. The Jews of Esther's day passed down this yearly celebration to their descendants in order to remember what the Lord God had done that day for his people.

Xerxes was rewarded by God for the favor he showed the Jews. He grew in wealth and power. Mordecai also grew in power in the land. The record of his service in Persia was written in the annals of the kings of Media and Persia. He was held in high regard by the Jews for his work on their behalf.

In the end, the Lord God overcame the enemies of his people. While God's people were in exile because of their sin, God still took care of them. There were times when God's people questioned his ways and purposes. There were times when the Jews could neither understand what God was doing nor see his purpose. God had not abandoned them in their hour of need.

I find it tremendously encouraging that all this took place as God's people were being punished by God for their rebellion against him. It was in the land of exile that the Lord met them in such a powerful way. This encourages me because I see that God will keep me even when I fall short of his standard. He loves me even when I sin. He will not abandon me because I have not perfectly served him. I often fall short, but God will always be faithful. How thankful we need to be.

God will never change. What he did for his people in the days of Esther, he will do for us today. He raises up those who seem insignificant and makes them people of tremendous influence. He reaches out to a less than perfect people and blesses them. As Esther and Mordecai stepped out in obedience and faithfulness, God opened up doors of opportunity and deliverance. I believe we can trust the Lord to do the same for us today.

For Consideration:

- What is Purim? How was it celebrated?

- What victories has the Lord God given you in your life? How have you demonstrated your gratitude to God for these victories?

- Have you ever found yourself questioning the purposes and plans of God for your life? Have things in your life ever become overwhelming? What does this chapter teach us about God and the victory he offers us?

- How important was the favor of God on the lives of Esther and Mordecai? Is the favor of God on his children today? How might we experience God's favor?

For Prayer:

- Thank the Lord for the victories he has given you in your life.

- Ask the Lord to forgive you for the times you have not trusted him and his purpose.

- Thank the Lord for the way he goes before us to open doors.

- Ask God to enable you to know his purpose and plan for your life. Ask him for strength and enablement to step out into that purpose.

Light To My Path
Devotional Commentary Series

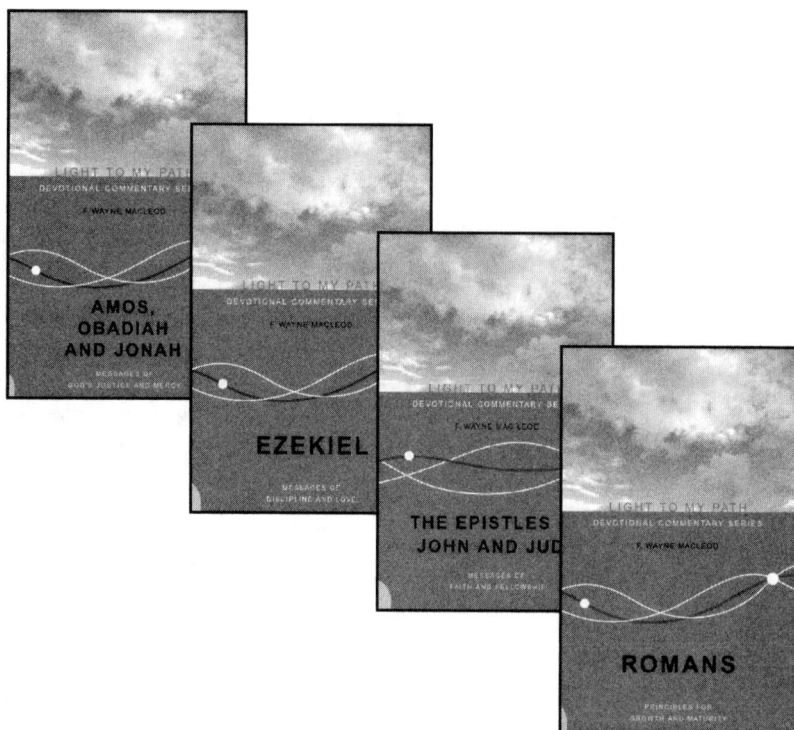

Now Available

Old Testament

- Ezra, Nehemiah, and Esther
- Ezekiel
- Amos, Obadiah, and Jonah
- Micah, Nahum, Habakkuk, and Zephaniah

New Testament

- John
- Acts
- Romans
- The Epistles of John and Jude

A new commentary series for every day devotional use.

"I am impressed by what I have read from this set of commentaries. I have found them to be concise, insightful, inspiring, practical and, above all, true to Scripture. Many will find them to be excellent resources."

Randy Alcorn
director of Eternal Perspective Ministries,
Author of *The Grace & Truth Paradox*
and *Money, Possessions & Eternity*

Watch for more in the series
Spring 2005

Old Testament

• Israel
• Haggai, Zachariah and Malachi

New Testament

• Philippians and Colossians
• James and 1&2 Peter

Other books available from
Authentic Media . . .

A
Authentic
MEDIA

PO Box 1047
129 Mobilization Drive
Waynesboro, GA 30830

706-554-1594
1-8MORE-BOOKS
ordersusa@stl.org

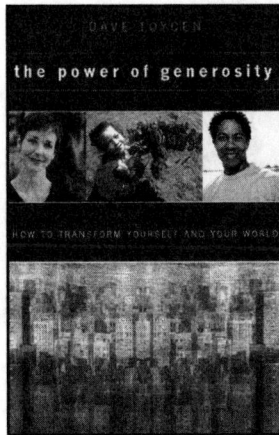

Power of Generosity
How to Transform Yourself and Your World

David Toycen

An intimate journey down the road of giving, *The Power of Generosity* will strike a chord with all who want to fulfill a vital part of their humanity–the need to give.

Dave Toycen, President and CEO of World Vision Canada, believes generosity can save lives—both the benefactor's and the recipient's. The act of giving without an ulterior motive inherently nurtures a need human's have for significance. During three decades of traveling to the poorest and most desperate countries, Dave has seen and met individuals who have been freed by acts of generosity.

What is generosity? What motivates a person toward benevolence? *The Power of Generosity* is a practical guide to developing a spirit of generosity, providing thoughtful answers and encouragement for all those looking for ways to be more giving in their lives.

1-932805-10-9   192 Pages

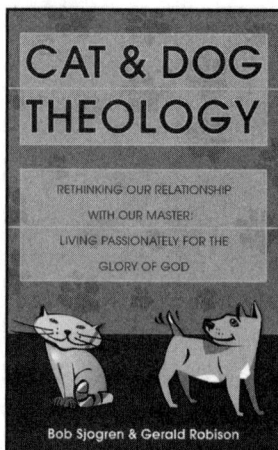

Cat and Dog Theology
Rethinking Our Relationship With Our Master

Bob Sjogren & Dr. Gerald Robison

There is a joke about cats and dogs that conveys their differences perfectly.

> A dog says, "You pet me, you feed me, you shelter me, you love me, you must be God."
>
> A cat says, "You pet me, you feed me, you shelter me, you love me, I must be God."

These God-given traits of cats ("You exist to serve me") and dogs ("I exist to serve you") are often similar to the theological attitudes we have in our view of God and our relationship to Him. Using the differences between cats and dogs in a light-handed manner, the authors compel us to challenge our thinking in deep and profound ways. As you are drawn toward God and the desire to reflect His glory in your life, you will worship, view missions, and pray in a whole new way. This life-changing book will give you a new perspective and vision for God as you delight in the God who delights in you.

1-884543-17-0   206 Pages

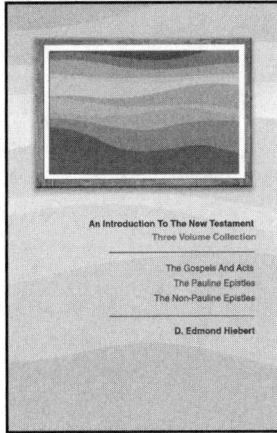

An Introduction To The New Testament
Three Volume Collection

D. Edmond Hiebert

Though not a commentary, the Introduction to the New Testament presents each book's message along with a discussion of such questions as authorship, composition, historical circumstances of their writing, issues of criticism and provides helpful, general information on their content and nature. The bibliographies and annotated book list are extremely helpful for pastors, teachers, and laymen as an excellent invitation to further careful exploration.

This book will be prized by all who have a desire to delve deeply into the New Testament writings.

Volume 1: The Gospels And Acts
Volume 2: The Pauline Epistles
Volume 3: The Non-Pauline Epistles and Revelation

1-884543-74-X   976 Pages